A Matter of Choice

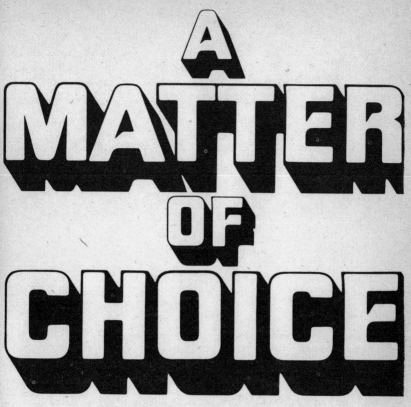

A MATTER OF CHOICE

Judson Edwards

BROADMAN PRESS
Nashville, Tennessee

© Copyright 1983 • Broadman Press
All rights reserved.
4252-04
ISBN: 0-8054-5204-4
Dewey Decimal Classification: 248.4
Subject Heading: CHRISTIAN LIFE
Library of Congress Catalog Card Number: 81-71493
Printed in the United States of America

Unless otherwise indicated, Scripture quotations are from the *New American Standard Bible*. Copyright © The Lockman Foundation, 1960, 1962, 1963, 1971, 1972, 1973, 1975. Used by permission.

Scripture quotations marked (KJV) are from the King James Version of the Bible.

Scripture quotations marked (Phillips) are reprinted with permission of Macmillan Publishing Co., Inc. from J. B. Phillips: *The New Testament in Modern English,* Revised Edition. © J. B. Phillips 1958, 1960, 1972.

Scripture quotations marked (RSV) are from the Revised Standard Version of the Bible, copyrighted 1946, 1952, © 1971, 1973.

To
Sherry, Stacy, and Randel
with the hope that our family
will always make
biblical choices

Acknowledgments

Writing a book is a lonely venture. Yet, every person who writes has been influenced by a multitude of people. My family and friends, whom I know well, and many authors, whom I have never met, have contributed to this book. To all of them I am grateful.

The Heritage Park Baptist Church, where I am privileged to serve as pastor, has been the anvil on which I have hammered and shaped the ideas expressed in these pages. To all who have made Heritage Park such a vibrant church, thanks for your spirit and the encouragement you have given me.

Finally, I must express my gratitude to Sarah Kay Brice for her superlative work in typing the manuscript and to Becky New for her careful proofreading of this material.

Introduction

Over nineteen hundred years ago, Paul counseled a group of Christians in Rome, "Do not be conformed to this world, but be transformed by the renewing of your mind, that you may prove what the will of God is, that which is good and acceptable and perfect" (Rom. 12:2). He was reminding those early Christians, in danger of being swallowed by a pagan society, that their commitment to Jesus Christ was a commitment to holy nonconformity. J. B. Phillips translated Paul's plea to the Romans in a graphic way: "Don't let the world around you squeeze you into its own mould, but let God re-make you so that your whole attitude of mind is changed." They were not to be squeezed and pressured into living like everyone else.

The call to follow Jesus Christ has always been a call to nonconformity. It was true for Romans in the first century, and it is the same for Americans in the twentieth century. In the Christian realm, priorities, relationships, and attitudes are radically different from those in the world-at-large. Jesus knew that, of course, and spoke of his way as a narrow way that most people would never find.

This book is an attempt to articulate some specific, tangible ways in which Christians are to be nonconformists. It contrasts society's message, as propagated in books, movies, advertisements, songs, and conversation-at-the-supermarket, with the biblical message, as propagated in the Old and New Testaments. Nine issues, ranging from money to sex to church, are examined and studied from both perspectives. The claims of the world are set forth and the counterclaims of the Word are then discussed. The purpose is to show how Christians are to be different from their comrades. You see, it is one thing simply to say, "Christians are different." It is another thing altogether to know precisely *how* Christians are different and to pinpoint nonconforming biblical mandates for everyday living.

Two dangers rear their ugly heads when one undertakes the task of "fleshing out" Romans 12:2 and trying to underscore the discrepancy between Word and world. The first danger is the tendency to become critical of and negative toward everybody who is not a Christian. It has always been easy to throw stones, but stone throwing seldom solves any problems. In the following pages, I will dwell on the positive aspects of the Bible rather than the negative aspects of society. However, anything truly prophetic has a tinge of criticism in it; so if I lapse into occasional stone throwing, simply lump me in with some of the biblical prophets who were at odds with the world.

The second danger is the tendency to focus on Christian works and, in the process, forget grace. Anytime we emphasize our works to the exclusion of God's grace, we are on the road to burdensome, legalistic Christianity. Certainly the Christian should follow specific commandments which spell out a different, unique life-style. But obeying those commandments does not earn God's love. As John reminded us in 1 John 4:19, "We love him, because he *first* loved us" (KJV, author's italics). All we do as Christians is in response to God's incredible grace. That grace motivates us to be different from the world around us. I hope you will see each chapter in this book as a joyful response to God's love and not a burdensome attempt to earn it.

The Bible still issues a clarion call for disciples to be nonconformists; to walk a narrow, sparsely populated road; to bet their lives on a message which seems to most of the world antiquated and irrelevant. If this book can somehow clarify the counterclaims of the Word, and if it can goad a few people to stake their lives on the truth of that Word, it will have accomplished its purpose.

Contents

1
Money:
Status Symbol or Tool of Love?

Contemporary American society has defined "the good life" as one which has the following five ingredients: youth, beauty, money, love, and health. So, most of us dash through life at breakneck speed trying to gather all five at the same time so we can declare ourselves "successful." The tragedy is that very few of us ever "get it all together."

The young man with a good measure of youth, handsomeness, and health, for instance, may well be lacking in loving relationships and financial stability. And in a desperate effort to find people to love genuinely and money for his account, that searcher-after-life ironically loses his youth, handsomeness, and health. By the time he sinks some roots into a few stable relationships and settles into a comfortable financial position, he has high blood pressure, a pot belly, and gray hair (or none at all!). But chances are the quest will not die easily and the middle-aged searcher will enroll at the spa to improve his health, revamp his wardrobe to enhance his appearance, and dye his hair, trying to recapture his youth. Men and women all over American are trying frantically to garner all five of the ingredients which make up the pie of successful living.

Of those five ingredients, though, only one stands a chance of being caught if chased persistently enough. That one is money. The other four seem to be mostly in the hands of providence, chance, or other people.

Youth cannot be caught, even with bottles of hair dye or designer clothing. It is a gift which quickly passes away.

Beauty can be pursued, but all of the makeup and fancy clothes in the world cannot overcome big ears and beady eyes. Beauty is mostly dependent on genes and chromosomes and is largely out of our control.

Health, too, is a fickle commodity that is hard to control. Even the most avid health fanatic is fair game for viruses, tumors, and freak accidents. Even daily vitamins and arduous jogging cannot guarantee disease-free living. Like youth and beauty, health is at the mercy of many factors beyond our own control.

And love? Love can also be chased, but it is far too dependent on other people to be classified a sure catch. We can give love only at the risk of deep hurt and frustration; for love, to be satisfying, must be returned to us by someone else. And there is never any guarantee that our love will be reciprocated.

No, only money is the product of our own initiative, insight, talent, and perspiration. The other four factors may be largely beyond individual control, but money is the one piece of the pie we can effectively manipulate. Quite logically, then, most of us give ourselves vigorously to the pursuit of the dollar. And in our culture, it is the one ingredient in "the good life" that, more than any other, signals the worth of our existence. Our ability to make and spend money boldly declares our "success" to the world. It gauges the extent of one's initiative, the brilliance of one's insight, the measure of one's talent, and the willingness of one to perspire.

Of course, this is nothing new. As far as I can tell, money has always been the prime indicator of a person's worth. Our generation is probably no different from those which preceded it. Like our ancestors, we have fallen on our knees to pay homage to silver and gold. But our infatuation with paper and coins has a decidedly modern thrust to it. Before we drift off to sleep at night, we read *How to Prosper During the Coming Bad Years* or *The Rich and the Super Rich* or *Dress for Success.* At the dentist's office, we thumb through *Money* magazine or *The Wall Street Journal.* On Sunday morning, the thick newspaper reminds us that, to be really happy, we need a condominium at Aspen or a Caribbean cruise. The sports page tells us of the superstar's dissatisfaction because he makes only half a million dollars a year. Always, in the back of our minds, there is the dream of moving from the crowded, three-bedroom house to the five-bedroom one in Chantilly Glen with the game room. We are literally surrounded by not-so-subtle hints that making and spending money is "where it's at." Somewhere I read, "If the love of money is really the root of all evil, God is not too pleased with America." We Americans do love our money!

An article in *World Vision* magazine likened us to the greedy fool on the hill who plays "Ostrich-in-the-Sand" while multitudes perish in the valley. The article delineated how the selfish person spends his money. That year in the United States for every one hundred dollars earned a percentage of that amount went to the following items:

- $18.30 went for food
- $ 6.60 was spent for recreation and amusement
- $ 5.50 was used for clothes
- $ 2.40 went for alcohol
- $ 1.50 bought tobacco
- $ 1.30 was given for religious and charitable uses

The ancient Hebrews believed in the tithe and invested a tenth of their earnings in the work of God. Modern Americans see money as a status symbol and are content to invest 1 percent of their income to aid others and 99 percent is spent on themselves.

Years ago, Charles Lindbergh saw with crystal-clear vision and spoke these prophetic words:

I grew up as a disciple of science. I know its fascination. I have felt the godlike power man derives from his machines . . . . Now I have lived to experience the early results of scientific materialism. I have watched men turn into human cogs in the factories they believed would enrich their lives. I have watched pride in workmanship leave and human character decline as efficiency of production lines increased . . . . We still have the possibility, here in America, of building a civilization based on Man, where the importance of an enterprise is judged less by its financial profits than by the kind of community it creates; where the measure of a man is his own character, not his power or wealth.[1]

Regrettably, though, that possibility has never become a reality, and we still judge a person—either consciously or unconsciously—more by his car and clothes than by his character.

And the church, commissioned to be an energetic dynamo of holy nonconformists, has itself been ensnared by culture's view of money and has often lost its prophetic role. The contemporary church has come to measure its success in terms of chandeliers, fleets of buses, and multimillion-dollar buildings. Too often now, the institutional church judges its success like big business gauges its success.

Colin Morris, a minister embroiled in the Anglican-Methodist Union debate in Zambia nearly two decades ago, was forced to scrutinize his own priorities and those of the church when a little Zambian man dropped dead of hunger less than one hundred yards from Morris's front door. While he and his clergyman comrades wrangled denominational politics, a man died of starvation. An autopsy revealed there were a few leaves and what appeared to be a ball of grass in the Zambian's stomach. That one incident drastically changed Morris's ministry.

After that experience, the importance of church debate, committees, and resolutions seemed trifling. The priority became the man with the shrunken belly and how to prevent that tragedy from ever occurring again. Morris clearly saw the gap which exists between the "haves" and the "have nots," the nearly uncrossable chasm that separates the corpulent cats on the hill from the starving ones in the valley.

> This is the great divide that no unity talk can bridge. Not between Christians and non-Christians, nor Catholics and Protestants, but between gluttons and paupers. And the judgement upon us is that we are an integral part of a gluttonous Church in a gluttonous society. We cannot speak to that other world because we are not even in it. We pursue our private obsessions whilst mankind is laid waste about us. Only the well-fed play at Church. The rest are too busy raking dust bins and garbage heaps for a morsel to feed their children.[2]

That great divide will never be bridged until the people on the hill grasp a totally new concept of money. As long as money is a status symbol, the chasm will only widen.

A parable John Claypool relates will serve to point up modern confusion about the purpose of money. Claypool tells of a young man who went to a personnel office to apply for a job. He was told he would have to take an aptitude test, was ushered into a large room, and told to complete the test in a certain amount of time. The man quickly became enamored with the utensils at his disposal in the testing room. He sharpened all of the pencils, shined the table, and straightened piles of paper. He became so engrossed in the things around him that he forgot to take the test! At the end of the allotted time, the personnel attendant returned to collect and grade the man's test, only to discover that the man never answered a question. The fellow didn't get the job!

That young man got his "means" and his "ends" confused. The table, pencils, and paper were put in the room to serve as the means to an end. They were the tools to enable him to take the test, but the applicant made the tools the prime focus of his interest. When "time was up," all he had to show for his efforts were sharpened pencils, a sparkling table, and a pile of paper.

The story sounds ridiculous, but that is the tragedy of the "average American." God has put us on earth to prepare us for life with him in eternity, to take a test which will equip us for heaven. But we have become so fascinated with cars, houses, vacations, and expensive trinkets that we have made them the end and purpose of life. Many of us no longer make money to live; we live to make money. And the heartbreak, of course, is that, in our preoccupation with things, we are failing the test God put us here to take.

What, then, does the Bible offer as an alternative to possession-mania and money as a status symbol? Is there a biblical stance regarding the use of money, and, if so, just how is a holy nonconformist to view his possessions? The Bible presents money as a tool of love. The concept of money as a tool to be used in loving other people is implicit in the Old Testament and extremely explicit in the New Testament.

Early in the Old Testament, the idea of money as a tool of love began to take root and work itself into the Word. Two Hebrew customs clearly show this Old Testament idea of money as an instrument of caring. Those two practices are gleaning and tithing. In Leviticus, God declared that the Israelites were to leave the gleanings of their harvest in the field:

> "Now when you reap the harvest of your land, you shall not reap to the very corners of your field, neither shall you gather the gleanings of your harvest. Nor shall you glean your vineyard, nor shall you gather the fallen fruit of your vineyard; you shall leave them for the needy and for the stranger. I am the Lord your God" (Lev. 19:9-10).

Early in their nation's life, God began to stress to the people of Israel that part of what they owned should be given to "the needy and the stranger."

The concept of the tithe further strengthened the idea of generous giving: "Thus all the title of the land, of the seed of the land or of the fruit of the tree, is the Lord's; it is holy to the Lord" (Lev. 27:30). A tenth of all they produced was to be given to God, and the failure to offer the tithe was tantamount to robbery (see Mal. 3:8-10).

There runs throughout the Prophets, too, a strong strain of concern for the downtrodden. The prophets proclaimed to Israel that money was not to be hoarded but freely shared with those in need. Two examples, one from Isaiah and one from Jeremiah, are typical of the prophets' pleas for generous giving. Isaiah on Israel's responsibility:

> "Is it not to divide your bread
>   with the hungry,
> And bring the homeless poor into
>   the house;
> When you see the naked, to cover him;
> And not to hide yourself from your
>   own flesh?
> And if you give yourself to the
>   hungry,
> And satisfy the desire of the
>   afflicted,
> Then your light will rise in
>   darkness,
> And your gloom will become
>   like midday" (Isa. 58:7,10).

Jeremiah on Judah's neglect of the poor:

> "Like a cage full of birds,
> So their houses are full of
>   deceit;
> Therefore they have become
>   great and rich.

> They are fat, they are sleek,
> They also excel in deeds of
>   wickedness;
> They do not plead the cause,
> The cause of the orphan, that
>   they may prosper;
> And they do not defend the
>   rights of the poor.
> 'Shall I not punish these people?'
>   declares the Lord,
> 'On a nation such as this
> Shall I not avenge Myself?'" (Jer. 5:27-29).

But the Old Testament merely lays the groundwork for what came in the New Testament. Prophetic utterances, gleaning, and tithing were but forerunners of a more explicit stewardship concept in the new covenant. With the coming of Jesus, God's desire that money be used as a tool of love is made plain.

In the Sermon on the Mount (see Matt. 6:19-34), Jesus declared that his followers do not build their lives on material things which are destined for decay. Their priority is God's kingdom and their investment is in God, not money. Luke's version of this portion of the Sermon on the Mount even includes the injunction to: "'Sell your possessions and give to charity; make yourselves purses which do not wear out, and unfailing treasure in heaven, where no thief comes near, nor moth destroys'" (Luke 12:33).

In Luke 12:15, Jesus specifically repudiated the popular idea of money as a status symbol: "Beware, and be on your guard against every form of greed; for not even when one has an abundance does his life consist of his possessions."

The priority of spiritual wealth over material wealth is again made clear in the Carpenter's haunting question recorded in Matthew 16:26: "For what will a man be profited, if he gains the whole world, and forfeits his soul? Or what will a man give in exchange for his soul?"

Jesus' encounters with Zaccheus and the rich, young ruler also shed significant light on the Lord's concept of "things." From all indications, Zaccheus was short, rich, and miserable. As a tax collector in Jericho, he made a tidy sum of money each week, some illegally. But money has never been able to purchase life, and Zaccheus scurried up the sycamore tree that day in a frantic, self-forgetting attempt to find another alternative. When Jesus stopped under the tree, called him by name, and accepted him, Zaccheus found what he was looking for.

Interestingly enough, the only change Luke recorded about the tiny tax collector was the one made in his view of money. After he met Jesus, Zaccheus pledged half of his possessions to the poor and promised to restore fourfold any money he had acquired illegally. I wish Luke had been inspired to record more of the conversation between the seeker and the Answer. Something took place between Zaccheus and Jesus that turned a money monger into a cheerful giver. Many of us need that same remarkable transformation within us.

After the encounter with Zaccheus, Jesus turned to his followers and told them the story of the nobleman who entrusted a large sum of money to each of ten slaves. Upon his return from a far country, the nobleman called for an accounting of his money. One by one the slaves had to reveal their use of what they had been given. The first slave reported that he had been able to increase the original amount by ten times. The second slave showed an increase of five times the initial sum. But the third slave, cautious and fearful of losing what he had, hadn't invested the money at all. He offered the nobleman the original amount neatly wrapped in a napkin. The irate nobleman chided his timid servant for not investing his money and then gave the sum to the slave who had invested most shrewdly.

In light of the episode with Zaccheus which prompted this parable, the kind of investment Jesus was referring to here is rather obvious. Zaccheus had changed his personal priorities and given lavishly to the poor and to those he had cheated. His investments were thus not in houses and lands, but in the needs of people. Then Jesus related the story of the nobleman and his slaves to underscore the importance of his followers' investing their goods and money in human beings as Zaccheus had. Those who have a Christlike concept of money take their wealth and give it without rancor to "the least of these." Thereby they are multiplying many times over what God entrusted to them. Those with a distorted view of possessions are like the fearful slave and have only a selfish spirit and a napkinful of trinkets to offer as returns on their lives' investments.

Jesus' encounter with the man commonly dubbed "the rich, young ruler" is recorded in Luke 18, the chapter preceding the dialogue with Zaccheus. This man, too, was a searcher, wondering how to find life and salvation. He had found money, success, and morality, but he still sensed a gnawing restlessness within himself: "'Good Teacher, what shall I do to obtain eternal life?'" Jesus pointed him first to the Ten Commandments, specifically the five Commandments that speak to relationships with other people. The ruler replied that he had been a card-carrying practitioner of such things ever since he was a boy.

Then Jesus probed him at the point of his money and made a stringent demand of him: "One thing you still lack; sell all you possess, and distribute it to the poor, and you shall have treasure in heaven; and come, follow Me" (Luke 18:22). Jesus wanted to see if the man were willing to use his money as a tool of love instead of a personal status symbol. Regrettably, the ruler was not ready for that kind of commitment and trudged back into his world of joyless wealth. "And Jesus looked at him and said, 'How hard it is for those who are wealthy to enter into the kingdom of God!'" (Luke 18:24).

It has always been hard for the rich to enter the kingdom, for society has always led them to believe that they are *worth* much because they *have* much. Society has always preached the status-symbol concept of possessions, and prosperous people are especially gullible targets for that false gospel. But Jesus will not let his followers buy that popular line. He insists that his disciples deny themselves and take up the cross and follow him. The ruler is welcome in the kingdom, but only if he adopts the same priorities as Jesus. And one of those is that money be used as a tool of love.

The ruler could not change his stance toward "things." Zaccheus somehow did. You and I, twenty centuries later, are offered the same terms. We will choose to hoard our money and see ourselves as worthy individuals because we have luxury cars or diamond pendants; or we will choose to share our money and see ourselves as useful people because we have fed the hungry or clothed the naked or sent an ambassador to point the lost the way Home. We will opt either for acquiring so we might live or for giving so others can.

Jesus said that if we want to know the passions and priorities we now have, there is a simple test we can take: "Where your treasure is, there will your heart be also" (Matt. 6:21). In essence, if you want to know where your heart is, look at your treasure. If you want to know your personal priorities, gaze no further than the stubs in the checkbook. Such a test may well reveal that many of us "good Christians" have some radical priority shifting to do. One truth is certain: if we are serious about making Jesus our lord, our possessions must become tools of love he can use in building his kingdom.

Most people will see you as a bit fanatical and strange if you choose to be biblical and not conform to the world's standards when it comes to your money. I'm sure Zaccheus got some raised eyebrows at the tax office the morning after he had made a spectacle of himself in the tree. But the words of Jim Elliott still make good sense to one who has glimpsed eternal things: "He is no fool who gives what he cannot keep, to gain what he cannot lose."

One of the ironies of Scripture is that Jesus was betrayed for money. He who lived and taught that money was a tool of love became the victim of a greedy disciple. Judas, the treasurer of the disciples, used money as a brutal bludgeon of hate. He was a traitor for thirty, shiny pieces of silver.

Those of us in the contemporary band of disciples also betray our Lord when we do not use our money as an instrument of love as He taught us. Judas, the ancient disciple, sold his allegiance for silver. I pray we modern disciples will not.

Notes

1. Quoted by Calvin Miller, *A Thirst for Meaning* (Grand Rapids: Zondervan, 1976), p. 34.

2. Colin Morris, *Include Me Out* (Nashville: Abingdon Press, 1968), p. 58.

2
Power:
Intimidation or Servanthood?

It was the kind of occasion that makes your eyes misty and your voice quiver. It was a supper celebration, but nobody really felt like celebrating. Impending death hung in the air like a murky fog; and if nobody talked about it, everybody was surely thinking about it. Jesus was going to die. He knew it, and his friends at the supper knew it too. The thought of death has a way of dampening any would-be celebration.

It was also the kind of occasion when one's entire life came into focus, a special time when parting words and farewell symbols were appropriate. Here, in the upper room, Jesus left his friends some visible insignia of his life. Here he told them, or showed them, the essence of his three-year walk with them. Here, before he died, he bequeathed to them the strategy and the power to carry on after he was gone.

I can think of many symbols we would expect a dying man to leave his loved ones. Jesus could have responded in a variety of ways to his impending death.

"*And after supper, he took a wad of money and treated his disciples to a merry time.*" The ancient Epicureans said, "Eat, drink, and be merry for tomorrow you shall die," and since Jesus really was going to die, why not enjoy his last hours on earth? Money has always been a symbol of power and pleasure, so why not leave in his friends' minds a picture of life at its merry best? However, it was not to be. Money was not the farewell symbol of Jesus' life.

"*And after supper, he took a chariot and fled into a far country.*"

This, too, would have been a logical response to the pressure and pain Jesus was facing. The chariot of escape could have carried him far away from Calvary to safer places. But escape from hardship never had been his approach, and he refused to run from his cross.

"*And after supper, he took a pen and wrote his personal memoirs for all the world to read.*" Any dying person would like to leave behind a tangible expression of his unique self. If not a book he had penned, then a picture he had painted or a poem he had written or a table he had handcrafted; but Jesus chose none of these for his farewell symbol.

"*And after supper, he took a sword and led a revolution against Rome.*" The disciples had waited three years for the Messiah to assert himself. Surely now, with his back to the wall, Jesus would display his divine power by leading them on a military rampage. The sword has always been a symbol of power, and if ever there was a time to show power, that celebration in the upper room was the time. But neither was the sword to be Jesus' farewell symbol to his followers. Peter would try to force that symbol upon him in the garden of Gethsemane, but once again Jesus would reject it.

As logical and sensible as all of those symbols are, the soon-to-be-crucified One rejected them all. The one symbol he chose to leave as a legacy is a shocking one:

> Jesus . . . rose from supper, and laid aside His garments; and taking a towel, girded Himself about. Then He poured water into the basin, and began to wash the disciples' feet, and to wipe them with the towel with which He was girded (John 13:3-5).

His farewell symbol was a towel! Imagine—the Messiah, God's Son, with a towel on his arm, stooping to bathe the dirty feet of his friends! What a surprising picture and what a paradoxical portrait of divine power!

It is, in fact, a portrait of power the world never has been able to see and understand. Power, from the world's perspective, has to do with domination and force, not with washing feet. Power is intimidation and clout, not servanthood and humility.

But the picture of Jesus on his knees before his friends with a towel in his hands and a basin by his side is not to be dismissed as powerlessness or foolishness. The picture of Jesus hanging between two crooks at Golgotha is not to be dismissed as weakness or foolishness either. In retrospect, those disciples who felt his hands on their feet in the upper chamber that evening saw those events as examples of the awesome power of God. Paul described that paradoxical power like this:

> But we preach Christ crucified, to Jews a stumbling block, and to Gentiles foolishness, but to those who are the called, both Jews and Greeks, Christ the power of God and the wisdom of God (1 Cor. 1:23-25).

After that evening at supper and after the events at Golgotha, the disciples understood better the meaning of the word *power*. It is time you and I come to grasp its meaning too.

Years ago Canon Streeter, a British preacher, defined power as the ability to accomplish purpose. That is a most helpful definition. Power is not power unless it can accomplish what is needed. By that definition, a shotgun is a powerful implement for fending off trespassers or downing flying quail. But when it comes to teaching a child how to count to ten, a shotgun is powerless. It cannot accomplish that feat. So, too, an ax is a powerful instrument for chopping wood. If you want a good shave, however, an ax is useless. A fragile razor that weighs an ounce has more power in that situation.

The definition of power as the ability to accomplish purpose helps us better understand the foot-washing episode in John's Gospel and "the power of the cross" (1:18) Paul wrote about in 1 Corinthians. Jesus' purpose on earth was to establish a kingdom of love and servanthood. To accomplish that purpose, the other farewell symbols at his disposal were powerless. Money could not buy such a kingdom. Intimidation could not force people into loving and serving. The only tools of power fit for such a task are towels and crosses! When Jesus girded himself and washed feet, he was showing those disciples the way to build a kingdom. When he carried a cross up a hill and died for wrongs he did not do, he was demonstrating the only kind of power that would accomplish his goal.

In his book *Who Goes There?*, J. Wallace Hamilton wrote about the two kinds of power in human relations:

> There are only two kinds of power in the area of human relations. One is coercion, the other persuasion. One is regimentation, compulsion from without. The other is devotion from within. One is power *over* people. The other is power *with* people.[1]

The popular concept of power is coercion, compulsion from without, power *over* people. Jesus' concept of power was persuasion, devotion from within, and power *with* people.

Those two kinds of power met head-on in the judgment hall when Jesus stood before Pilate. Pilate's view of power was the popular one that has existed throughout the ages: "Do you not know that I have power to release you, and power to crucify you?" (John 19:10, RSV). Jesus' view of power was different: "My kingdom is not of this world. If My kingdom were of this world, then My servants would be fighting, that I might not be delivered up to the Jews" (John 18:36). There he stood, deserted by his friends, facing a torturous scourging, displaying the only kind of power strong enough to build God's kingdom: the power of sacrificial love.

Pilate could not comprehend that power; and two thousand years after the Man with the towel on his arm and the cross on his back, we don't understand that kind of power either. We still define power in terms of intimidation, force, and control. If you don't believe it, merely browse through your local book store and look at some of the self-help books on the shelves. These books, written to show us how to be "successful" human beings, are prime examples of the world's concept of power. I recently looked through a book store at a shopping mall and noticed how many of the popular self-help manuals deal with the issue of power and how to get more of it. Here are a few of the titles that grabbed my attention: *Winning Through Intimidation, How to Become an Assertive Woman, Power* ("This book will get you a bigger raise, a better job and total control over everyone around you."), *The Art of Selfishness, Getting Yours, Assert Yourself,* and *Looking Out for #1.* Somehow those titles don't seem to match the philosophy of Jesus, who not only washed feet and gave himself away but also prescribed that same life-style for anyone serious about finding deep-down living. The self-help treatises claim we win through intimidation; the gospel declares we win through servanthood. The world recommends power through assertiveness; the gospel suggests power through submissiveness.

This power through submission and servanthood is advocated in both the Old and New Testaments. Long before the Messiah was born in a stable, some of the Old Testament prophets began to see that power as control and domination would not build God's kingdom. In Isaiah 53, for example, the issue is the power of God. The prophet asserted that God would unleash his mighty power in the person of a Suffering Servant:

> Who has believed our message?
> And to whom has the arm of the Lord
>   been revealed?
> For He grew up before Him like a
>   tender shoot,
> And like a root out of parched
>   ground;

He has no stately form or majesty
That we should look upon Him,
Nor appearance that we should be
    attracted to Him.
He was despised and forsaken of men,
A man of sorrows, and acquainted with
    grief;
And like one from whom men hide their
    face,
He was despised, and we did not
    esteem Him.
Surely our griefs He Himself bore,
And our sorrows He carried;
Yet we ourselves esteemed Him stricken,
Smitten of God, and afflicted.
But He was pierced through for our
    transgressions,
He was crushed for our iniquities;
The chastening for our well-being
    fell upon Him.
And by His scourging we are healed.
(Isa. 53:1-5)

Jeremiah also saw that power from without would not suffice in accomplishing God's purpose. So, he spoke of a new kind of power that would be released "inside" the hearts of people, to woo them and draw them to God:

"But this is the covenant which I made with the house of Israel after those days," declares the Lord, "I will put My law within them, and on their heart I will write it; and I will be their God, and they shall be My people" (Jer. 31:33).

In a violent world marked by scores of bloody military battles, the prophets began to hint at another kind of power—the power of God and his people to suffer and to reach humanity through love.

That power became most visible hundreds of years after the prophets in a dingy stall at Bethlehem. There Almighty God made his entrance into humanity, not as a military warrior on a black stallion, but as a fragile baby in a bed of straw. And from that humble beginning, the baby went on to live a life that boldly declared the emergence of a new power, the awesome power of vulnerability and servanthood. He dined with outcasts and sinners, healed the brokenhearted, loved the unlovely, shunned material gain, washed feet, and hung on a cross to show the world, once and for all, the only kind of power that can accomplish God's eternal purpose.

When he inaugurated his ministry before the home folks at Nazareth, Jesus chose to describe his role this way:

> The Spirit of the Lord is upon Me,
> Because He anointed Me to preach the
>   gospel to the poor.
> He has sent Me to proclaim release to
>   the captives,
> And recovery of sight to the blind,
> To set free those who are downtrodden,
> To proclaim the favorable year of the
>   Lord (Luke 4:18-19).

The Messiah "did not come to be served, but to serve, and to give His life a ransom for many" (Matt. 20:28).

Years later when Paul wrote to the Philippians, he admonished them to unleash that same power of servanthood in their community:

> Have this attitude in yourselves which was also in Christ Jesus, who, although He existed in the form of God, did not regard equality with God a thing to be grasped, but emptied Himself, taking the form of a bond-servant, and being made in the likeness of men. And being found in appearance as a man, He humbled

Himself by becoming obedient to the point of death, even death on a cross (2:5-8).

The call to us today is an urgent summons to have Christ's attitude of servanthood. Our power is not based on bullying, domination, or manipulation. Like our Lord, we are to take on "the form of a bond-servant" (Phil. 2:7), and make the towel and the cross the symbols of our daily walk.

To do this we need to know how a commitment to power-through-servanthood will actually manifest itself in our daily relationships. We cannot be content to speak of being servants in general. We must make some specific commitments in tangible situations or all of our talk about servanthood is only the pious babbling of hypocrites. How will this kind of power manifest itself in our lives?

Colin Morris entitled one of his provocative books *Include Me Out*. Anyone who makes a personal decision to become a servant will have to say "include me out" to some of the world's frantic pursuits.

"Include me out," for example, of the power struggle within my own family. I am no longer going to battle for dominance and control and try to get what is mine. Instead, I am going to be a servant to my spouse and my children. The key question is not going to be, How can I be happy today? It is going to be, What can I do to make my family happy and fulfilled today? I am going to move from a position of dominance, irritability, and frustration to a stance of submission, peace, and enjoyment. I am going to make Paul's advice to submit "yourselves to one another" (Eph. 5:21, KJV) the motto of our family's life together.

"Include me out," too, of the popular dash for status, money, and clout in the business world. I no longer need to pull strings or bully people or cut corners to climb the ladder of success. I will choose instead to enjoy what I do, to use my abilities creatively, to be honest on the job, and to look for ways to make life better for those with whom I work.

"Include me out" of relationships marked by competition and conquest. In my relationships, I no longer have to prove that I am witty, intelligent, or without problems. In Christ, I am now free to be myself, in love with my Lord and my friends, and trying to prove only that I care. I will talk less and listen more. I will move the spotlight off of myself and put it on others.

Because of my commitment to power-through-servanthood, "include me out" of arguments over rights, the concept of money as status symbol, the pleasure-at-any-price philosophy, morbid preoccupation with my own problems, and anything else that would keep me from being a slave to and for Jesus Christ.

Three characteristics are necessary to become a person with a servant heart. As we seek to develop these three characteristics in our lives, we will find that we will be able to serve more effectively and to better unleash the power of Christ in our world.

A Servant Looks for the Best in Others

Jesus called tempestuous Simon a "rock" and changed his life. He called Zaccheus "a son of Abraham" and had supper with him. He conversed with the adulterous woman at the well and, in doing so, affirmed her worth as a person. His ministry was very much one of seeing and calling out the best in each person he met. Those who would imitate his style will also look for the best in people. Worldly power looks for imperfections to exploit; Christian power looks for strengths to call forth. Someone once commented, "See a man as he is, and he will remain as he is. See him as what he can become, and someday he will become it." Anyone who will have a servant's heart will eliminate criticism and negativism and see people in the light of what they can become.

A Servant Is Genuine

Servant power follows closely on the heels of honesty and transparency. People are liberated in the presence of someone who recognizes his own humanity and dares to express it. False piety and imitation perfection only serve to drive people away and destroy any hope for real communication.

The truth, according to the Bible, is that all of us are "weirdos"—oddballs, misfits, and sinners. And the ones who will release the power of selfless love into the world are those who dare to admit their weaknesses, those who will be genuine and real. Sometimes we humans, like our Divine Maker, have to lead from weakness instead of strength.

A Servant Takes Hold of "the Near Edge"

As mentioned earlier, real servanthood is specific and concrete. The person who will display the "power of the cross" is the one who grabs "the near edge" of some problem and does whatever possible to remedy it. Until we move from the general to the specific, we will never release any power.

Our problem is not world hunger, for example. Our problem is that we've not even taken the individual first step of tossing our widow's mite into the kitty. Our problem is not that our world is lost without Christ. Our problem is that we've never grabbed hold of "the near edge" and spoken the good news to our neighbors. Our problem is not that millions of people are sick unto death with loneliness. Our problem is that we don't have time to visit the aged widow who lives down the street.

The people who will find servant power will be the ones who, like the Suffering Servant himself, take hold of individual people and situations and try to make a difference there.

I believe that anyone who tries to call out the best in others, is genuine and real, and who gets intimately involved in specific needs will be on the verge of finding the kind of power explosive enough to move the world toward God.

Many in our day will see this servant concept of power as foolishness. Like those first-century skeptics who scoffed at the cross, they will see servanthood as pitiful and humility as weakness. The dollar, the bomb, and the corporate machine will continue to reign as symbols of modern power. The towel and the cross will be seen as tools only for mad people and fools. But those of us who have lashed our lives to the Word of God know that we have found the only power potent enough to make a new world. And we cling tenaciously to Paul's words to the Corinthians: "But God has chosen the foolish things of the world to shame the wise, and God has chosen the weak things of the world to shame the things which are strong" (1 Cor. 1:27).

The symbols of other religions suggest beauty and light: a six-pointed star, a crescent moon, a lotus. The symbol of Christianity, the cross, is a symbol of death. It suggests that power is not at all what we think it is.

Note

1. J. Wallace Hamilton, *Who Goes There: What & Where Is God* (Old Tappan, New Jersey: Revell, 1958), p. 137.

3

Happiness:
Gratification or the Gospel?

No book in the Bible better captures the mood of modern America than the Book of Ecclesiastes. The theme of the book is the pursuit of happiness, and that seems to be the theme of life in our society. People desperately want to be happy! The mood of Ecclesiastes, however, is far from gaiety and celebration. In fact, the writer of the book was cynical and pessimistic. He tried all of the recommended steps to happiness and finally found only disillusionment.

First, he tried pleasure; but wine, women, and song did not fill the aching need within him. So he turned to wisdom and became a learned man, only to discover that knowledge does not automatically bequeath happiness either. Finally, he tried wealth and surrounded himself with "the finer things of life," only to find that money and things have little to do with lasting joy. What was his conclusion after dashing down the roads to bliss? "'Vanity of vanities! All is vanity'" (1:2). He tried all of the prescribed recipes for happiness and came up as hungry and haggard as ever.

I think the preacher in Ecclesiastes has a lot of company in today's world. Many of us have dashed down the road to bliss and have experimented with the same things the Old Testament searcher tried. But pleasure didn't satisfy. Learning only left us bewildered, and money bought us everything but genuine joy. Now we join with him and sing in unison our mournful tune: "Vanity of vanities! All is vanity."

What do people do when they've run along the road to bliss and have failed to catch the elusive emotion called *joy?* Many become desperate in attempts to escape the vanity and futility of their searches. Some opt for drugs, others hard liquor. Some try divorce. And the awfully desperate ones commit suicide. One only has to read the newspaper or glance at the current statistics to see how many have despaired on the road to bliss.

There must be an alternative, though, that could help us in our search for personal happiness. If pleasure, wisdom, and wealth are vanity, there must be something that "works." Surely the Bible must speak about how people can latch onto happiness and ride with it a lifetime.

Fortunately, Jesus did utter a few choice words on the subject; but they are so strange-sounding, we've never taken them very seriously. In the Beatitudes (Matt. 5:3-12), he drew a picture of a happy person, and it is quickly apparent that Jesus' view of happiness (blessedness) and the popular view are vastly different.

The popular concept of happiness is the same one the writer of Ecclesiastes had. That is, you "find" happiness by pursuing it. You chase after pleasure, learning, and money because, when you finally track them down, personal contentment is the real prize. In the Beatitudes, Jesus came at happiness from the opposite direction. He suggested that we don't find happiness but that, if we will live in a certain manner, it will someday find us. He seemed to indicate that happiness is a by-product, a serendipity, of specific life qualities and that if persons will pursue the development of those qualities they stand a good chance of being overtaken by joy.

Let us take a careful look, then, at Jesus' concept of happiness as revealed in Matthew 5. Perhaps we will be more shocked and disturbed if we contrast his view of happy living with the popular idea of happiness. Jesus made eight statements about happiness and who the happy people are, and every one of these declarations contradicts the world's standards of successful living.

> **POPULAR VIEW #1:** Happy are the proud who have all of the right answers and keep all of the religious rules, for they shall have a good image.
>
> **JESUS' VIEW:** Happy are the poor in spirit, for theirs is the kingdom of heaven.

Image is a popular word today, and most of us will do anything to preserve those precious facades we have built. How frantically we try to present good fronts to others! To the world, the unpardonable sin is revealing chinks in our spiritual or emotional armor or displaying imperfections in our personalities. Personal pride places a mask before our faces and keeps us from being honest and genuine in our relationships, both with God and people. We cannot admit who we are, even to ourselves. We cannot reveal our true identities!

Jesus said, rather shockingly, that the happy people are not the proud with the good images, but those who are "poor in spirit." This phrase carries the idea of humility, complete dependence on God, and an honest recognition of one's spiritual bankruptcy apart from God. It means we are made humble as we recognize who we are and then we assume an open stance of vulnerability and servanthood in the world.

Jesus told a story which vividly describes the meaning of being "poor in spirit" (see Luke 18). It is the story of the religious Pharisee and the sinful publican. The Pharisee, filled with pride and self-sufficiency, a man determined to keep his "image," prayed a pious prayer, thanking God that he was not like the publican. The publican, filled with repentance and humility, a man destitute apart from God, prayed a nonreligious prayer for forgiveness. Ironically, the publican—that desperate but genuine man who was "poor in spirit"—went home justified. And ironically his attitude toward life is the one which leads to happiness. This publican recognized who he was, showing his real self openly to the world and depending solely on God. That, in a nutshell, is what it means to be "poor in spirit."

> POPULAR VIEW #2: Happy are those who never have problems and losses, for they will have no worries.

> JESUS' VIEW: Happy are those who mourn, for they shall be comforted.

A young mother leaves her two-year-old child with the baby-sitter. Upon her return, the question she invariably asks is, "Have you been good while Mommy was gone?" Now, what this question really means is, You didn't write on the walls, did you? You didn't break anything, did you? I hope you didn't bite the baby-sitter! What she means is, You haven't been too bad, have you? In her mind, goodness is equated with not being bad. Goodness is the absence of badness.

We frequently measure happiness similarly. Happiness, we think, is the absence of problems. As long as there are no major problems looming in the horizon, we assume happiness will naturally follow. Hence, we are somewhat perplexed when the circumstances surrounding us are smooth and untroubled, but inside we feel a boredom and a restlessness we certainly would not call joy: *things are going so well, I wonder why I'm not happy?*

Jesus rather abruptly jolted the people's thinking when he said, "How happy are those who know what sorrow means, for they will be given courage and comfort" (5:4, Phillips). Perhaps of all of the Beatitudes, this one is the most paradoxical. How can a mourner possibly be happy?

Jesus was saying, in this remarkable little sentence, that

truly abundant living does not occur in a vacuum. Happiness is something that happens in a world of sickness, death, evil, and confusion. It is a quality of life quite distinct from events and circumstances. The really happy people live in a fallen world of problems and loss but find there a Source of strength and love that adds a new dimension to life. This Resource in the midst of tragedy, this Strength in the midst of loss, this Comfort in the midst of death, gives the mourner a perspective and insight into life that can only lead to deep happiness and confidence. One realizes that ultimately nothing can defeat one if God is at the center of one's being. With Paul, a person can say, "I can do all things through Him who strengthens me" (Phil. 4:13).

The happy person is the one who mourns; for, in the darkness, he will find God, he will be comforted, and life will never be the same.

POPULAR VIEW #3: Happy are the ambitious and the arrogant, for they shall push their way to the top.

JESUS' VIEW: Happy are the meek, for they shall inherit the earth.

Winning through intimidation is a common theme in American society. We have been taught that those who succeed scratch, claw, manipulate, and dominate. A win-at-any-cost attitude permeates our culture. Influenced, no doubt, by our fanatic interest in sports, we now believe that a life of victory goes to the one who "hits the hardest" and never lets up.

Once again, Jesus overturned the tables of success. He stated, "Blessed are the meek: for they shall inherit the earth" (5:5, KJV). This statement, taken from Psalm 37, is another strange-sounding dictum that leaves us reeling. What did Jesus mean?

The word *meek* is usually misunderstood to be a synonym for *timidity* or *cowardice*. In reality, the word connotes the idea of gentleness and patience. It implies a personality that is not showy or external. One Bible commentator has said that the word prohibits revenge, irritability, and being overly sensitive in personal relationships.

Perhaps there is no better picture of meekness in the New Testament than that of Jesus standing before Pilate. In that encounter, Jesus showed gentleness, kindness, patience, and courage, but there is no trace of cowardice or timidity. In the face of pressure and wrong, he responded with grace and forgiveness. He showed there the meaning of meekness as power under control.

This attitude of meekness, very similar to being "poor in spirit," means that we recognize who we are in the light of who God is. Such a realization moves us away from pride and impressiveness to an attitude of humility and complete dependence on the Father. We no longer have to push and climb. We no longer have to dominate and manipulate. We are free to be ourselves, God's servant-people, in a world marked by self-pride, manipulation, and artificiality. This quality of meekness, translated into our warped culture, would be a strange and glorious thing to behold.

Happiness belongs to those rebellious, nonconforming souls who dare to be meek.

POPULAR VIEW #4: Happy are those who hunger and thirst after possessions, for they shall have the "fine things" of life.

JESUS' VIEW: Happy are those who hunger and thirst after righteousness, for they shall be filled.

American society is afflicted with a rampant epidemic of possession-mania. Materialism is certainly our trademark. If happiness is often measured by an absence of problems, it is also often measured by the presence of possessions. Real happiness to many is having a lot of "things."

In bold contrast to our frantic quest for worldly goods, Jesus said that the happy people are those who strive toward righteousness. All of that energy expended in securing "things" could be rechanneled down the avenue of righteous living. Righteousness is a theological-sounding word which means, quite simply, "being and doing what is right." It is a broad word which covers and includes honesty, integrity, and loving relationships. Righteousness, as Jesus used it here, implies a striving to be all God created us to be. Notice that this desire for righteous living is not merely a casual matter of dropping into church, giving to a favorite charity, or being a "nice" person. It is a "hungering and thirsting," a deep longing, a constant pursuit, a style of life. It is a serious striving toward Godlikeness.

It is good news that such striving is not futile, for the hungering-and-thirsting one will be "filled." This filling, I am sure, is not a sudden, once-for-all satisfaction but a gradual, continual experience. As one moves toward God—in attitudes, relationships, and actions—yearning for life and meaning is satisfied. Righteousness pays dividends, for it "fills" that emptiness and lostness within us.

A serendipity awaits the striver for righteous living and Godlikeness: He is surprised by joy!

POPULAR VIEW #5: Happy are those who watch out for themselves, for they shall not be exploited.

JESUS' VIEW: Happy are the merciful, for they shall obtain mercy.

In terms of our relationships with others, we fall into one of two categories. We are either self-centered or other-centered.

Certainly, we vary in degrees between total self-centeredness and total other-centeredness, but these two broad classifications can help us refine our focuses in life. *Does the spotlight of my interest and love fall on myself or others?*

By far the vast majority of people, I have noticed, focus the spotlight on themselves. Their time, money, and energy are expended for personal satisfaction. They do not set out to be callous and unkind. They do not see themselves as selfish or unloving. They just don't happen to notice the needs of others. Life has a way of numbing our awareness; and quite unconsciously, we become insensitive to people. We can visit, work, and even live with people who are hurting and fail to detect the throbbing pain in their lives. We have been so conditioned to believe that happiness is a matter of attaining personal goals and achieving personal success that we are frequently blind to the needs of others. We are firmly convinced that happiness will come as we garner "prizes" for ourselves—money, power, and reputation.

So, we are stunned again when we read that Jesus said that the really happy people are the ones who have their focus on others. "Happy are the merciful," those who have concern and compassion for people, those who are sensitive and aware of those around them.

The Lord showed us the meaning of the word *mercy* in his story of the good Samaritan. It is the story of three men—two with the spotlight on themselves, one with his eyes opened to see others. The first two travelers might have been concerned with all of the things that "tie us up" today, such as, important business meetings, church activities, and family plans. They hurriedly bypassed the wounded man on the roadside. The third man, the Samaritan, stopped and showed the stranger "mercy." He saw his need, took the time to deal with it, and did what he could to help. This merciful Samaritan literally gave of himself, and Jesus concluded the story with a plea to "Go, and do thou likewise" (Luke 10:37, KJV).

Happiness means moving toward other-centeredness, and the One who faced a cross for others reminded us to move the spotlight off of ourselves. "Blessed are the merciful" (5:7). It's a paradox, isn't it? To find life, we must give it away.

POPULAR VIEW #6: Happy are those who sin, for they shall know real pleasure.

JESUS' VIEW: Happy are the pure in heart, for they shall see God.

"Eat, drink, and be merry, for tomorrow you shall die," we still hear today. We have accepted raw hedonism as the philosophy that leads to real living. Seeking pleasure at any cost, living for "kicks," getting our "thrills"—we have made happiness a by-product of momentary pleasure. If you don't believe we are Epicurean and hedonistic, look at how Americans spend their money. We chase pleasure at any price! We have been beguiled by the Serpent into believing the notion that pleasure—godly or ungodly, moral or immoral—is the target at which we are to shoot. If an adulterous sexual escapade leads to momentary ecstasy, pursue it, and you will be happy. As one song went, "If it feels good, do it." If drugs or alcohol provide fun for the crowd, join in, and find fulfillment. If you have the money, buy plenty of pleasurable playthings, for they will dispel boredom and lead to ultimate joy. We have been led to believe that momentary pleasure, and even sin, bring lasting happiness. The Beguiler has spun his hedonistic web around America, and we are trapped and floundering in our own patterns of living.

Of course, this philosophy might not be too bad if life ends at death, if this is the only moment for which we live. Why not sin, why not step on others, why not seek pleasure as the priceless pearl if there is nothing beyond us, if there is no God? But Christians believe in an eternal life. Jesus, the One who came from beyond, tried, throughout the Sermon on the Mount, to equip people to live for eternity. His perspective was otherworldly and his goal, to equip people for life in that world with his Father. So, he cannot go along with our popular view of happiness. He said the happy person is not the sinful pleasure-seeker who basks in his fleeting thrills. The happy person is the one who is "pure in heart" (v. 8).

In contrast to the external, bodily purification so important to the Pharisees of that day, Jesus taught that happiness depends on the purity and cleanliness of one's inner being. The person who has pure motives and intentions, the person who acts and lives out of an honest and clean spirit, is the person who finds joy in life.

This teaching leaves us gasping, for what one of us will ever achieve such purity and innocence? Aren't most of our deeds, even the good ones, colored with stains of personal pride, self-gain, and other impure motives? Surely this is true, but Jesus gives us a different goal and target. Happiness will not be found in sin, wrongdoing, and momentary pleasure. Happiness will be found when, in the presence of God's continual forgiveness and remolding, our spirits are cleansed and purified. Such cleansing, such continuous re-creation, such striving to be pure within, yield joy and fruitful living. The happiest people in the world are those who live pure lives out of pure hearts.

When all the returns are in, sin really doesn't pay, but striving for purity of thought, attitude, and spirit pays off in the dividend of happiness.

POPULAR VIEW #7: Happy are those who never get "involved," for they shall be independent and carefree.

JESUS' VIEW: Happy are the peacemakers, for they shall be called the children of God.

The word *peacemaker* connotes the idea of a reconciler, one who makes peace between enemies. It has to do with breaking down the walls and barriers that separate and divide people. The task of the "peacemaker" is the very task of God himself: "God . . . hath reconciled us to himself by Jesus Christ" (2 Cor. 5:18, KJV). God breaks down the partitions that separate us from him and then bids us to be his reconciling agents in the world: "[He] hath given to us the ministry of reconciliation" (2 Cor. 5:18, KJV).

There are countless "walls" which splinter and fracture our society. Prejudice splits us into the light-skinned and the dark-skinned. Poverty divides us into the haves and the have-nots. Ignorance divides us into the learned and the unlearned. Even our religion fragments us into sects and denominations with subsequent feelings of competiton and jealousy between groups. Jesus was saying that his true followers are the ones who assume the God-like work of being peacemakers, of breaking down the barriers which separate people.

Contrary to the prevalent belief that security and happiness follow closely on the heels of detachment and uninvolvement, Jesus said that the happy people are those who are actively involved in bringing God's peace to a troubled world. The happy life is not found in the security of the camp, but in the danger and excitement of the front line. The happy person is not the comfortable one with folded hands, but the concerned one who reaches out to bring peace to another.

Perhaps some walls have been erected right where we are: between family members, work associates, friends, or churches. Our personal happiness depends, to a large extent, upon our willingness to become involved in destroying those walls.

POPULAR VIEW #8: Happy is the one who follows the crowd, for he shall be accepted and popular.

JESUS' VIEW: Happy is the one who is persecuted for the sake of righteousness, for his is the kingdom of heaven.

There has been much talk, in recent years, about "doing your own thing." I have noticed, however, that in spite of this so-called liberating philosophy, the "herd instinct" is as strong as ever. Kierkegaard once commented that "The crowd is untruth," but not many believe him. We still follow the crowd and try to live just like everyone else. I suppose we will continue to worship society's values and goals as long as we are convinced that therein lies the path to happy living. Happiness, to some, is thinking and living exactly like those around us. Woe be to the individuals who are different!

This "herd instinct" is probably one reason Jesus' Sermon on the Mount is so disturbing to us. Throughout the sermon, the Master destroyed comfortable ideologies and society-influenced standards of successful living. Some are annoyed because this One didn't see life as we see it. His concept of real living is so radical and strange! This last Beatitude is so typical of his unbelievable philosophy of life. He said that happiness lies not in popularity and public acceptance, but in rejection and persecution. "Blessed are they which are persecuted for righteousness' sake" (v. 10, KJV). What kind of philosophy is that? What could he possibly have meant?

This unusual Galilean, who himself was eventually rejected and persecuted, was saying that joyful living is something quite different from conformity to worldly standards. In fact, it is the antithesis of that. Happiness comes when a person has been set free to step to the beat of a "different drummer." Real living comes when a person is free to let God be God, regardless of the consequences. Jesus, who continually rejected the world's way to travel God's way, teaches us that following God, not the herd, is actually the route to this life we are seeking.

Those who are persecuted for the sake of righteousness are happy because they have been freed from the world's dizzy search for meaning. They have found a Higher Allegiance, a life-changing, all-encompassing Father; and in their oneness with him, they have found lives worth living.

In the past I have read many books in my quest for happiness: books by the dozens on how to be a success, how to know lasting joy, and how to live to the fullest. I have never read anything else like these strange teachings of Christ. His eight insights into happiness and a life of joy are unique. True, in these brief statements, we do not have an exhaustive study of what it means to live happily. However, Jesus did sketch an outline of a happy person for us. He quickly painted a mosaic of joy, and from his fleeting statements, a picture crystallizes in our minds:

(1) Happiness is an attitude of humility and vulnerability.
(2) Happiness is facing problems and tragedy, and finding a Father's hand in the darkness.
(3) Happiness is discovering power through gentleness and genuineness.
(4) Happiness is a "becoming," a moving toward Godlikeness.
(5) Happiness is giving your life away, a shifting of your focus to others.
(6) Happiness is a moving toward the goal of purity of attitude and spirit, as well as action.
(7) Happiness is being a peacemaker and bringing estranged people back together.
(8) Happiness is stepping to the beat of a different drummer, a radical obedience to God.

Jesus, in these Beatitudes, points us in a new direction on our journey down the road to bliss. His words do not answer all of our questions; and, in our desperation, we long for more detailed instructions. We long for a road map, but all we have are some new directional arrows along the roadside. Maybe, though, if we become desperate enough, we'll follow these divine arrows into unexplored regions. Maybe somewhere along that new avenue, happiness will find us, giving us what we have searched in vain for years to find.

4

Sex:
Cheap Thrill
or Celebration of Commitment?

"Contrary to Mrs. Grundy, sex is not sin. Contrary to Hugh Hefner, it's not salvation either. Like nitroglycerine, it can be used either to blow up bridges or heal hearts."[1] The Bible has a pertinent word for both the Mrs. Grundys and the Hugh Hefners. To Mrs. Grundy, heavy on propriety and condemnation, it offers a word of celebration. To Hugh Hefner, founder of the *Playboy,* it speaks a word of commitment. You see, Mrs. Grundy probably doesn't know that sex can be celebration. And Hugh Hefner doesn't seem to know that sex is empty without commitment. But the Bible both knows and declares that God intended sex to be both celebration *and* commitment. In fact, sex is to be a continuing celebration of the commitment a man and woman, in married love, have for each other.

In our day, the "Hefnerites" outnumber the "Grundyites." Or, if that is not the case, at least Hefner's disciples are more vocal. Sexual liberation is a resounding battle cry in today's American society. Thomas Howard explains the words of the popular battle cry this way:

Under the new myth there has occurred what is being called a sexual revolution, in which brittle and frightened ideas which plagued other generations are being examined and discarded. The idea that energizes this re-examination is that sexuality is a normal and natural function of healthy people, that it contributes to the richness of human experience, and that adults can very well make up their own minds as to how they will understand and use

53

this component in their make-up. There is a deep suspicion of the taboos with which other generations surrounded the phenomenon.[2]

To these modern minds trying to shed past taboos, Mrs. Grundy is a prude, a throwback to the Victorian age. But she too has her followers, and many of them reside in evangelical Christianity. Before confronting Hefner's sex without commitment, we would do well to give at least passing notice to Mrs. Grundy's sex without celebration.

Calvin Miller must have been where I have been because he precisely described the impressions I had about Christian sexuality when I was growing up. He wrote:

> I viewed the typical evangelical family as sitting around stiffly reading commentaries, talking in "churchese," and seeking the Holy Spirit's leadership before kissing "good night." To me, it all seemed so Spirit-led, so antiseptic and liturgical. It was as proper as a baptismal formula, as diplomatic as a board meeting. It was love that wanted to growl in hunger, but inhibited itself in the name of being Christlike. It was love that wanted to snuggle, but only shook hands.[3]

Though it is never articulated (talk of sex is of course forbidden), the philosophy of sex exuded by many evangelicals is one that is both repressive and ugly. In an honest desire to battle pornography and promiscuity, these well-meaning Christians give the impression that sex is evil and that sexual pleasure is the unpardonable sin. Instead of enjoying the gift of sex and using it as a vehicle to celebrate their love, some couples live in self-made prisons of inhibition and sexual stoicism.

The antidote to celebrationless sex is a clearer understanding of the Bible. Nowhere in God's Word is there any hint that sex is not to be enjoyed. In fact, the writer of Genesis declared that

God, after creating man and woman as sexual beings (male and female), pronounced his handiwork to be delightful. "And God saw all that He had made, and behold, it was very good" (Gen. 1:31). The Song of Solomon is essentially a poem extolling the joy of romantic, sexual love, and some scholars believe the book was a manual of instruction for young Hebrew women. It certainly ought to be required reading for Mrs. Grundy!

So, I suspect the ancient Israelites knew they were to enjoy their sexual relationships. The danger, as most of the biblical material on sex reveals, was that the joy of being sexual creatures could be destroyed by the misuse of sex. Arguments from silence are always precarious, but volumes of biblical passages in praise of sexual celebration may be lacking for the simple reason that they were not needed. The pressing word for Jews of old was not "learn to enjoy sex," but rather "learn to use sex wisely!" That is still a sorely needed word, but let us not so magnify it that we make sex less pleasurable than God intends it to be.

Those Christians who have never been able to affirm and enjoy their sexuality have missed one of God's greatest gifts to them. If they have based their rigidity and repression on the Bible, they have been guilty of faulty interpretation. The biblical injunctions against some forms of sexual expression are given to *increase* joy, not to take away from it.

So, Mrs. Grundy needs to know that sex is celebration. She needs to understand that sex is a priceless gift from the Creator to give people both love and fulfillment.

It is probably true, though, that our society, like the ancient Hebrews, is more often guilty of sex without commitment than sex without celebration. Hefner's army now outnumbers and out-advertises Mrs. Grundy's. Examples of random sex, infidelity, and "liberation" in songs, movies, television programs, and books are too many to ennumerate. It is now thought quite stylish in contemporary America to be "free" enough to "swing" or "swap" or "experiment." There's a better than average chance that our Hollywood hero or heroine has been married four times and currently lives in a penthouse with a new lover. We have become a hoodwinked generation that believes perfect strangers will, and ought to, become perfect lovers if only someone will turn out the light.

Underlying this "freed-up" concept of sex is a whole bundle of assumptions and presuppositions. The sexual liberation movement has a gospel just like any other movement, and we need to examine the foundation upon which the "Hefnerites" have built their philosophy.

Youth and Beauty

The Liberation View

At the beginning of chapter 1, I delineated the five pieces in the pie of American success: youth, beauty, money, love, and health. Liberation sex places a premium on all five, but youth and beauty are especially vital. Undergirding our contemporary view of sex is the principle that people are sexy and worthy if they are young and attractive.

Everything from the television toothpaste commercial to the latest magazine ad for designer jeans accentuates the importance of being young. Of course, youth is and ought to be a time of exuberance, love, and vitality. But that truth blown out of proportion creates a serious crisis in the lives of the no-longer-young. It suggests that once a person has moved into mid-life, he or she has somehow lost something in terms of worth. Contemporary sex is pictured as a game for the young, and the impression is left that once the flower of youth has faded a person can no longer "play the game" very well. So, people spend thousands of dollars battling Father Time to present an illusion of youthful zest. *If* the popular myths about sex and youthfulness are true, that money is not a bad investment.

Beauty is also crucial to the modern concept of sex. Those paraded before us in movies, advertisements, and magazines are "the beautiful people": women with svelte figures, smooth skin, and toothpaste smiles, and macho men with handsome features and brawny physiques. The idea projected, though seldom verbalized, is that beauty is indispensable to success and popularity. As James Dobson wrote in *Hide or Seek*, beauty has become the "gold coin" of human worth. Without it, a person is doomed, or so we think, to a life of rejection and self-loathing.

And those responsible for selling their products capitalize on this passionate desire for attractiveness. As Dobson wrote:

> Any advertiser worth his salt knows that sex and beauty are the sensitive nerves on which to romp, and he must somehow link his products to those motivations, regardless of how contrived the connection might be. . . . There is no way to estimate the number of dollars spent each year to make us more competitive in an eroticized society.[4]

This, naturally, creates no small consternation within most of us. We know full well that age is creeping, or maybe galloping, up on us. We also know that our noses are crooked, that our legs are chubby, and that our breath is not always minty fresh. Though we hate to admit it, we know, deep down, that we are not "10"s. Therefore, we look in the mirror and feel a rising sense of panic. Youth is vanishing, and beauty, if it were ever present at all, is tagging along with it. Our worth, under the new sex scheme, is too frail to stand up to time. Dobson captured our plight when he wrote:

> It is my view that the increased sensuality in America during the seventies is generating a higher incidence of emotional casualties among people who are intensely aware of their inability to

compete in the flirtatious game. If beauty represents the necessary currency (the gold coin of worth), then they are undeniably bankrupt.[5]

The Biblical View

In sharp contrast to the popular concept of youth and beauty as components of personal worth, the Bible points us in two different directions. First, it indicates that "God sees not as man sees, for man looks on the outward appearance, but the Lord looks on the heart" (1 Sam. 16:7). And second, it states that pleasing God, rather than pleasing people, is the ultimate goal of life. In other words, Scripture offers modern people a different attitude and a different audience.

The attitude advocated by the biblical writers is that people should develop their *inner* beings. The Bible does not stress hints on grooming, advice on fashion, or behavioral ploys to make ourselves alluring to others. What we *will* find throughout the Bible are mandates for enhancing our inner selves: how to rid ourselves of guilt, what it means to love, how to have a life-sustaining faith, and where to go to find a peace that passes all understanding. Because God is concerned with the heart over the outward appearance, as the Lord told Samuel (Sam. 16:7), the Bible focuses on humans' "insides." When Paul wrote that bodily exercise is of little value, he was not so much condemning our morning jog around the block as he was suggesting that we get our priorities straight. Like the other biblical writers, his slant was always toward the inner self.

The biblical concept of worth centers on who people are rather than what they look, sound, or smell like. To all of us who may never make it as one of the "beautiful people," this message is sweet music. It points us to an attitude of seeking to be God's genuine person rather than society's fabricated one.

This biblical attitude draws its motivation from the Bible's concept of "who" the audience of life is to be. People should seek to develop their "hearts" because God, not other people, is the final judge of our success. "Liberated sex" says youth and beauty are crucial because what *others* think is all important. Scripture teaches that faith, hope, and love are crucial because what *God* thinks is all important. It offers us freedom from the rat race of successism, peer pressure, and one-upmanship that characterizes our society. For the follower of Jesus, God is the audience of life and seeking first his kingdom is top priority.

In summary then, underneath the random, flippant view of sex so much in evidence now, there is the disturbing belief that youth and beauty are priceless currency in today's "swinging" world. But the Bible continues to remind us what it has whispered to those generations which preceded us: You have a different attitude, for your focus is on the heart. And you have a different audience, for you are living before a crowd of One.

Certainly, I will try to look my best and will seek to avoid any signs of approaching old age. I will dress reasonably well, blow-dry my hair, and play tennis enough to stay slim. The quest for youth and beauty will occupy more of my attention than it probably should. But I will not build my worth on those fleeting commodities, and I will never bow down and worship them as gods. I hope I will have the good sense to build my life on the attitude and audience held up in the Bible and, therefore, seek to develop the inner man my Father desires.

Desire

The Liberation View

As the quote from Thomas Howard I used earlier states, many now see sex as a normal and natural function of healthy people and thus fair game for anyone who desires it. This warped view has it that the only prerequisite to sex is passion, and desire is viewed as the sole passport needed to enter the arena of sexual bliss.

Obviously, human beings have a need and a desire for sexual relationships, and this desire is totally normal in the confines of marriage. But to warp that truth and make it claim that all sexual desires should be fulfilled is ridiculous. Sex is not like a ham sandwich one devours whenever he is hungry. It is a physical and mystical union between a man and a woman who want to express their commitment and love to each other. Ham-sandwich sex soon leaves a person empty and frustrated because it nullifies the very purpose and reason for having a sexual relationship in the first place.

The Biblical View

The Bible indicates that people are created in God's image, only a little lower than the angels. Therefore people are, or should be, above animal-like responses to life. People don't have to act only on impulse. Our minds, rather than our glands, should steer our courses. Whenever we lower ourselves to doing whatever we desire, we destroy our true humanity. One biblical writer said, "The things which they know by instinct, like unreasoning animals, by these things they are destroyed" (Jude 10).

Personhood

The Liberation View

Since desire is the only ticket needed in the new sex concept, people become objects whose purpose is the satisfaction of another's desire. This mentality demeans personhood and pictures people as objects for self-gratification. This is one of the most devastating assumptions of "Hefnerism." Men and women are seen only through eyes of self-centeredness and exploitation.

Andy Warhol, in his autobiography, expressed this vantage point when he wrote, "Brigitte Bardot was one of the first women to be really modern and treat men like love objects, buying them and discarding them. I like that."[6]

The criteria for a modern relationship becomes not integrity or kindness or devotion, but whether one can "score" with the opposite sex. Sex is the focal point of the relationship, and such other pursuits as understanding, listening, and learning to care are forgotten. In this scheme, people are walking sex objects whose most pressing need is to find some other desperate sex object who is willing to go to bed. Liberated sex sees people as "playmates" and "pets," never as flesh-and-blood humans who need to know and be known.

The Biblical View

In the Sermon on the Mount, Jesus forbade his followers to lust. The problem of lust is the very one I am describing here. It is a distorted way of looking at another person. It prohibits the selfless, loving relationships Jesus wants us to have with others. Lust, viewing another person only as a sex object, is forbidden because Christ will not allow us to see people as pawns in a selfish quest for self-gratification. Anytime we look at people with emploitive eyes that ask, Can you satisfy my needs? we are not walking the same road the Suffering Servant walked. Therefore, no lust and no liberated-sex mentality either.

In the biblical view, people are sexual creatures, but they are more than that. They have the capacity to learn and love and actually to be earthen vessels that reflect the divine image. So, people are never objects to be used for pleasure. They are "thoughts of God," in Helmut Thielicke's words, who need to know other humans in depth.

Any philosophy that posits people as objects to fulfill

personal needs for pleasure desecrates the meaning of the word *human*. And the "new sex," motivated more by lust than love, does precisely that.

Commitment

The Liberation View

The "new sex" is sex without commitment. It is sex detached from covenant, a random coupling of any willing parties. This view goes: If a person finds another attractive (young and beautiful preferably), if a person has a strong desire, and if a willing object can be found to fill that desire, then it is only normal to get together sexually. Commitment is never mentioned as an ingredient in the pie.

The Biblical View

The Bible makes commitment the prime ingredient. It is impossible to comprehend the biblical material on human sexuality apart from the concept of commitment. The old word used occasionally in the Bible to picture a sexual relationship is the word *know*. Adam "knew" Eve, and Cain "knew" his wife. In the Bible, sex is always related to "knowing." In the context of a sexual relationship, a man and a woman "know" each other in the fullest sense, and their commitment to each other is renewed.

Even when polygamy was the practice in the Old Testament, sex was still tied to commitment:

> Solomon had three hundred wives and seven hundred concubines, but there was no mistake about whose they were; they were the king's, and let the rest of you jolly well keep your hands off. Even here there was a committal: The king took it upon himself to provide for his harem. . . . The committal that preceded the sexual union was that you both give yourself to me and take me, and I do likewise vis-a-vis you. This agreement is then enacted bodily.[7]

Only when we look through the eyes of commitment do we adequately understand what the Bible says about sex. Adultery is wrong because it is a violation of the marriage contract and commitment. The practices called "fornication" and "lasciviousness" in the King James language are wrong because they detach sex from a covenant to another person. Divorce is wrong because it shatters a sacred agreement. Only adultery is mentioned as reason for divorce; and in the case of adultery, the covenant has already been broken. Everything the New Testament speaks about sex is in the context of a warrant of love between a man and a woman. Every scriptural admonition on sex is a piece of lumber held up and supported by the foundation of personal commitment.

The modern concept of sex as a cheap thrill to be experienced whenever and wherever possible stands in sharp contrast to the Bible's lofty and consistent claims for sex. Anytime those lofty and consistent standards are not achieved, the purpose and the joy of sex are desecrated.

What much of society calls liberation, the Bible calls desecration. Sex can be fulfilling and enriching only when it is an outward symbol of an inner commitment.

So, the Bible certainly does speak to both of the modern views of sex so prevalent today.

It offers the playboys and playgirls a more joyful approach to sex than they can even imagine, one built upon the solid foundation of commitment.

It speaks to the "Grundyites" too; for, contrary to what they believe, sex *is* supposed to be celebration.

And before all of us it parades a high and holy view of sex: sex is the delightful celebration of a serious and specific commitment to the man or woman we love.

Notes

1. Frederick Buechner, *Wishful Thinking: A Theological ABC* (New York: Harper & Row, 1973), p. 87.

2. Thomas Howard, *Chance or the Dance?* (Wheaton, Illinois: Harold Shaw Publishers, 1979), p. 116.

3. Calvin Miller, *That Elusive Thing Called Joy* (Grand Rapids: Zondervan, 1975), pp. 105-106.

4. James Dobson, *Hide or Seek* (Old Tappan, New Jersey: Fleming H. Revell, 1974), p. 32.

5. Ibid, pp. 32-33.

6. Andy Warhol, *The Philosophy of Andy Warhol (From A to B and Back Again)* (New York: Harcourt Brace Jovanovich, 1975), p. 51.

7. Howard, pp. 126-127.

5
Church:
Bureaucracy or Koinonia

The question all of us in the Christian church must face is: Are we shaping the world or is the world shaping us? If we are honest, the answer to that question makes us fidget.

It is obvious from the New Testament that God's *ecclesia* ("called-out ones" in the Greek) began as a ragtag bunch of nobodies whose primary tool was a foolish willingness to be radically different from those around them. Because of what those early Christians saw and experienced in Jesus Christ, they banded together as nonconformists to show their world a new manner of life. They ate together, sang their spiritual songs, shared their material goods freely, openly loved, and confidently preached Christ in the marketplace. They were effective, not because of intellect or numbers or organization, but because they were fueled by a spirit of holy nonconformity. That early band of disciples ignited a *koinonia* of Christianity that affects us nearly two thousand years after the flame first flickered.

I do not think it advisable that we try to duplicate the first-century church in our day. In the first place, we cannot be the first-century church because we live in the twentieth century. Ours is a truly different world. In the second place, a desire to go back to past experiences is a veiled denial of the fact that God continues to work in history and may want his church to be doing new things. And, in the third place, judging by the New Testament, at least some of those early churches were none too exemplary. I doubt that Paul would ask that we copy the Corinthian church or that Jesus would have us mimic the Laodiceans.

But I do believe we must recapture a bold attitude of nonconformity if we are going to make a difference in our world. The modern church, like the first one, must become a *koinonia* instead of a bureaucracy, if it is to be the loving, witnessing, worshiping body God intends it to be.

The temptations our churches face today are many and varied. There are a multitude of obstacles that could trip us and keep us from becoming brush fires of contagious Christianity. Three temptations seem to be especially destructive, and the modern church seems to be unusually adept at stumbling over these three hurdles.

The three temptations, surprisingly, are the same ones Jesus had to face before he began his public ministry. The tempter dangled these temptations before Jesus and tried to lead him astray. But Jesus refused to succumb to these satanic ploys and came out of the wilderness with direction and conviction that propelled him to a lonely death. Like Jesus, the modern church must face up to the temptations of materialism, sensationalism, and compromise and, having turned our backs on them, move out into the world with renewed direction and conviction.

Materialism

In Matthew's description of Jesus' struggle in the wilderness, the first temptation was for Jesus to turn stones into bread. "And the tempter came and said to Him, 'If You are the Son of God, command that these stones become bread'" (Matt. 4:3). I think this was a temptation for Jesus to become a materialistic messiah, to base his strategy on physical needs. How popular any messiah would be if he could turn stones into bread and provide for the physical needs of humanity! This temptation offered our Lord a popular reign, a successful career, and a ministry built upon the demands of the people for satisfaction.

However, Jesus would not yield to this alluring suggestion. "But He answered and said, 'It is written, "Man shall not live on bread alone, but on every word that proceeds out of the mouth of God"'" (Matt. 4:4). The basis of Jesus' approach would not be popularity, success, and satisfaction, but rather a proclamation and an enactment of the Word of God. He did not give in to the temptation to be a materialistic messiah.

The modern church has heard this same temptation and has not been nearly as adamant in rejecting it! The temptation to be successful in worldly terms has been too much for many of us, and we have unconsciously fallen to the tempter. He has suggested that we objectify our ministries so we can measure our success in tangibles. In our evangelical heritage, this suggestion has led to an emphasis on what we jokingly call "the three *B*s": budgets, buildings, and baptisms. Now, there is nothing wrong with subscribing a budget or maintaining a lovely building or baptizing scores of people. Those are good in themselves, but the tempter always uses good things to trick good people. There was nothing wrong with turning stones into bread either, but Jesus knew that kind of objective act was not to be the trademark of his ministry.

So, too, we must always be sure that people, individual people with individual needs, are the cornerstone of our churches' ministries. The church does not exist to have a healthy bank account; it exists to spend itself and its money on people. The church does not exist to build and maintain buildings; it exists to use its resources in building a kingdom not made of mortar and stone. The church does not exist to round up herds of people and baptize them to outdo First Church downtown; it exists to call people into exacting, selfless discipleship, and then to baptize them as a symbol of that new life.

The ever-present danger is that, in our desire to be "successful," we will forget about people. And, of course, the

tempter is thrilled when we succumb to society's concept of
success. He surely knows that money, bricks, and wet bodies do
him no harm. But how he must quake when the church sets about
the business of seeing, knowing, and evangelizing specific
persons.

Let us be honest and admit that, in the contemporary
church, the three Bs *are* important. Without budgets and money
we cannot do much. Without buildings we lose some of our
identity and some of our programs. Without baptisms we lose our
zeal. But let us always be sure that, in stressing the Bs, we have
not stumbled over the hurdle of worldly success. It is such an
alluring temptation to long for impressiveness, be wealthy, and
project an illusion of effectiveness.

What we must always do, to fight off the temptation of
materialism, is ask the right questions. In addition to asking,
How many people show up here on Sunday? we must also ask, Is
anybody here becoming more like Christ? In addition to, Are we
meeting our budget? we must also ask, Are we really doing any
ministry? In addition to, How many have we baptized this year?
we must ask, How many of those baptized have we seriously
discipled? And always the question must be asked, Is there love
among us?

I might add that there is also an "un-success" band in the
modern church that seeks to be unsuccessful in terms of external
indicators. Rightly sensing the church's tendency to stumble into
materialism and successism, this group downplays any signs of
prosperity. For those in the "un-success" group, buildings are evil,
budgets are bureaucratic, and too many baptisms are a sure sign
of manipulation.

While I cannot number myself with this group, I know that
the tempter also comes too frequently to suggest that we turn the
stones into bread and then take a bow because we've been what
the world calls successful. Very quickly any church can become a

religious version of a corporation, gloating over facilities, profits, and the large number of customers who come through the door.

To his world, Jesus looked like a failure. By any earthly standards, he was not a success. He never made a fortune, wrote a book, or won a political election. He chose instead to love a few people deeply, to be true to his Father, and to give himself for a sinful world.

When the church is tempted to turn stones into bread and become impressive and materialistic, it should only have to read again of its Founder to right its course.

Sensationalism

The next temptation Jesus faced was the suggestion that he do something sensational and attention-getting. The tempter took him to the top of the Temple in Jerusalem and told him to prove his messiahship by jumping to the ground. Quoting a psalm, the devil indicated that God would send angels to rescue the true messiah, and the whole world would then have authentic proof that Jesus was the Son of God. Imagine the stir such a stunt would have caused in Jerusalem! Such a sensational, spectacular feat would have launched Jesus on a headline-grabbing ministry. However, the Messiah did not fall prey to the lure of a life built on the sensational. He left the desert of temptation with a firm conviction to make costly love and individual people the trade-marks of his ministry.

The temptation is still whispered to the corporate body of Christ to avoid costly love and to focus on big, splashy, spectacular events and programs. The church all too often succumbs to the notion that sensationalism is next to godliness. Thus, our buildings cannot merely be clean and functional; they must be breathtaking monuments that astound the community. Our eschatology must be graphic and colorful, and we must be able to surprise the world with our predictions concerning "the last things." In fact, in theology as a whole, sensationalism is the vogue. The books that sell and the preachers who are in demand are those with the most dramatic presentations of the Christian message.

But it is in our methodology that we most succumb to sensationalism. Preachers have swallowed goldfish when attendance records are set. Prizes are offered to those who can recruit the most visitors for the revival. Santa Claus rides the church bus to attract the neighborhood children, and many churches look for a big-name celebrity to feature on "Star Sunday" every year. We have fallen for the satanic ploy that equates sensationalism with effectiveness in our methods, and sacrificial love has been crowded off the church calendar.

Calvin Miller wrote about the modern bent toward salesmanship and sensationalism when he described the philosophies of some of the fast-growing churches in our country:

> I appreciate the rapid growth of evangelistic churches, but I am often stunned by their shallow philosophies. They are steeple-deep in charisma and methods. Listen to their Mardi Gras salesmanship, and you can tell that Christ is involved in the merchandising, along with other "fringe benefits." In one day you can leave the church with a coloring book, a kite, a doughnut, even a baptismal certificate, and an autographed picture of Brother Bob. Later it is clear that kites and coloring books are the most prized items, for baptismal certificates and pictures of Brother Bob litter the bus ramps.[1]

In a sincere desire to make the gospel attracive to the world, these churches forget that at the heart of Christianity there stands an unattractive cross which symbolizes costly love. When our sensationalism obscures that cross, we have unintentionally denied our Lord.

The biblical admonitions to pray, to give money, to visit the sick, to feed the hungry, and to tell others about Christ are not especially spectacular. One who takes those admonitions seriously will not garner headlines or gain fame. But Jesus both taught and lived that faithfulness in small things is the key to building his kingdom. His church must always remember that and then give itself in some unspectacular, but essential, ways to the task of redeeming the world.

Let us not be boring in our worship services. Let us never be afraid of innovation and experiment. Let us not give the impression that ours is a somber Way with no color or intrigue. And let us not be afraid to laugh and make merry when we come together at the church.

Let us also remember, though, that sensationalism is not the answer to the most pressing needs of humanity. Those needs can be met only when we come down from the pinnacle of the Temple and rub shoulders with people as Jesus did.

Compromise

The final temptation Jesus faced in the wilderness was to compromise and worship the devil. "Again, the devil took Him to a very high mountain, and showed Him all the kingdoms of the world, and their glory; and he said to Him, 'All these things will I give You, if You fall down and worship me'" (Matt. 4:8,9). "Just once," the tempter was whispering, "compromise your allegiance to your Father and do it my way." It was a suggestion Jesus would hear throughout his brief ministry. The pressure to compromise his convictions would face him almost continuously:

The Pharisees wanted him to conform to their legalistic approach to religion.
The crowds wanted him to satisfy their desires and meet their demands.

His own friends wanted him to conform to their image of
who a messiah was and how a messiah should act.
Pilate wanted him to compromise his claims to divinity
and, in doing so, escape the cross.

Everywhere he turned, Jesus heard the tempter's alluring
invitation to compromise. But Jesus had settled the issue in the
wilderness and would not deny his calling. "Then Jesus said to
him, 'Begone, Satan! For it is written, "You shall worship the
Lord your God, and serve Him only"'" (Matt. 4:10). The motto
of Jesus' life became "seek first the kingdom of God and His
righteousness," and nothing, not even a cross, would make him
be untrue to that standard.

The church cannot forsake that standard either, even if
holding it up means the Sunday School attendance drops. If, in a
sincere attempt to reach people and gain members, the church
compromises its gospel, whatever success it achieves is not
genuine Christian success. But the tempter is alive and well in
our churches, whispering his age-old message of a watered down
gospel. Too many of us, in our desire to grow, fall for it. As James
Smart contends, too often

> this emphasis upon growth leads easily to a lowering of standards,
> so that people are swept into the membership of the church
> without any adequate preparation for it, without any clear
> confrontation with the claims of the gospel and so without any
> real decision of faith.[2]

When we fail to hold up the standard of seeking first the
kingdom of God and his righteousness, the church testifies, in
Richard Niebuhr's words, to "a God without wrath, who brings
men without sin, into a kingdom without judgment, through a
Christ without a cross." Ours becomes a pseudo gospel that
makes Christ a cuddly teddy bear.

Follow Me

Our marching orders, both as individuals and as churches, are spelled out by Jesus in Luke 9:23: "If anyone wishes to come after Me, let him deny himself, and take up his cross daily, and follow Me." Our commitment, then, involves (1) a denial of self, (2) a daily decision, and (3) a definite direction. Without these three components, an individual's commitment and the church's proclamation are but cheap imitations of genuine discipleship.

A Denial of Self

This one ingredient alone makes the Christian message unpopular in our day. From many different sources in our society, we learn what we are to do with self. We are told to analyze it, assert it, love it, protect it, and improve it. Not many sophisticated moderns advocate denying it. So Jesus' mandate to deny ourselves seems to be out of step with the mood of our day. Surely our new understanding of the human psyche has moved us beyond the primitive notion of self-denial!

If so, followers of Jesus will gladly admit to being primitive. We are aware that real joy comes when a person can forget self in a higher cause. We recognize that a "primitive" commitment to follow Christ is an open recognition that self is not adequate, that self is sinful, that self needs direction. We know that such a commitment acknowledges the importance and necessity of simple obedience. And we know that our commitment will not be well received in a "self-ish" world. As Colin Morris wrote,

> This idea of the Christian life as a life-long convenant of obedience to Jesus is both too simple and too hard to be given much house-room in a world where consumer satisfaction is the test of everything; where we can always get our money back if we are not pleased with what we have bought.[3]

The person who rightly comes to Christ comes not to be satisfied or to get a spiritual thrill or to be blessed. He or she comes to deny self and to obey. But the exciting irony, discovered by many followers, is that in denying self, true self is discovered in a new and deeper way.

A Daily Decision

The decision is to take up a cross. This phrase does not mean bravely facing up to unpleasant situations. Taking up a cross does not mean smiling through hay fever season or enduring the misery of a constantly grumpy spouse. When Jesus declared we are to take up a cross daily, I think he was stressing that his followers must choose every day to give themselves, to sacrifice, to forget themselves in loving others. The cross is the ultimate picture of self-giving, and the decision to become Christian obligates a person to a life-style of serving and selflessness.

When a man and woman commit themselves to each other in marriage, they are legally husband and wife at the end of the initial ceremony; but they must decide daily whether they are truly married. In like fashion, when persons make an initial commitment to Christ, those decisions assure them a relationship with God. But those persons must then decide daily whether they will choose a cross, whether they will be like Christ.

The decision to live for others, to serve, runs counter to our natural, self-centered bent. Given the choice between contentment and a cross, the overwhelming majority of people will decide for contentment. But Jesus' followers are required to take up a cross daily; and, though it may be unpopular news, that requirement cannot be compromised. Christians are unique because of their meeting place. Daily, they gather around a cross.

A Definite Direction

The invitation Jesus gives is, "Follow me." Luke 9:23 is just one of several places where Jesus offered this invitation. He spoke it to Peter and Andrew by the Sea of Galilee. He said it to Matthew at the seat of customs. To a hesitant inquirer making excuses, he said, "Follow me; and let the dead bury their dead" (Matt. 8:22, KJV). To the young ruler, after suggesting that he sell his goods and give them to the poor, Jesus offered that same two-word invitation.

The words *follow me* can be spoken only by one who is going somewhere. Unlike the bumper sticker I've seen which reads "Don't follow me—I'm lost," Jesus indicated that he is going somewhere and invites us to move in that direction with him. The Greek word translated "follow" comes from the same root as the word "road." Jesus says, in effect, "Come share the road with me. I'll give you direction."

That initial decision to receive Christ places a person on the road with the Lord. It does not assure that the new convert will ever get off of square one however. A look at the membership rolls of our churches typically reveals that half of the members are uninvolved or unaccounted for. That statistic doesn't mean that all of our absent members are spiritually stifled, but it probably means that most of them are.

We must make it clear that the salvation experience is the end of a relationship with Christ—*the front end*. If we do not emphasize the "followship" of Christ, square one on the road will continue to be overcrowded, and our churches will be filled with disillusioned disciples jogging in place. Christ wants us to *follow* him, to be moving in a definite direction.

Anytime we fail to make clear the stringent demands of Jesus, we cheapen the gospel. We must always preach and teach and live denial of self, a daily decision to take up a cross of service, and a definite direction toward "followship" and maturity. When we fail to tell and live these truths, we have compromised our message and cast our lot with the tempter.

The temptations to be materialistic, to be sensational, and to compromise biblical truth will continue to face today's church. However, like its Founder, the church can grapple with those temptations, reject them, and then renew its determination to be a community of biblical nonconformists. We in the church can still choose to live, not by bread alone, but by the Word of God. We can still choose to shun the temple of spectacular religion for unnoticed deeds of caring. We can still refuse to bow before the devil and hold up the demanding, life-encompassing claims of our Lord.

If and when we make these decisions, the church will move away from bureaucratic institutionalism and will once again be the *koinonia* of love God intends it to be.

Notes

1. Calvin Miller, *A View from the Fields* (Nashville: Broadman Press, 1978), p. 90.

2. Quoted by Findley B. Edge, *A Quest for Vitality in Religion* (Nashville: Broadman Press, 1963), p. 202.

3. Morris, pp. 49-50.

6
Salvation:
Worldly Wisdom or the Folly of the Cross?

Humpty-Dumpty sat on a wall;
Humpty-Dumpty had a great fall;
All the king's horses and all the king's men
Couldn't put Humpty together again.

The pressing questions anyone in a Humpty-Dumpty world faces is: Who or what *can* put the pieces back together again? In a world of tragedy, conflict, sin, and discouragement, is there any hope for freedom from fragmented living? In a fallen world, who or what can bring salvation and wholeness?

The word *salvation*, as used in the New Testament, means "to be rescued" or "to be made sound." It has both present and future connotations. As we will see in the next chapter, salvation has an eternal dimension that ensures the Christian a confident future beyond the grave. But salvation also means rescuing from emptiness and lostness in the present. It is the difference between life and death *today*. Salvation, in the present tense, is the process by which Humpty-Dumpty people become whole again.

Where then does a person look to find this salvation in the here and now? The answers given to that all-important question are many and, to the average seeker, confusing as well. Society promises wholeness, "rescue," "soundness" in a number of ways; the Bible makes a persistent claim that salvation can be found down only one road. Let us look at three of the ways our society suggests that we find wholeness and then turn our attention to the biblical assertion.

Salvation: Society's Way

Salvation Through Psychology

One way modern people seek to find salvation is through psychology. In the last twenty years or so, psychology has moved from the black couch in the psychiatrist's office to the tweed one in the family room. Nearly every semi-educated American now has some expertise, either real or imagined, in the field of psychology. We now know of Freud, Maslow, Rogers, Erikson, Glasser, and Brothers. Transactional Analysis, est, assertiveness training, and self-actualization are terms with which many of us have at least passing knowledge. Psychology is no longer seen as simply a scholarly discipline for the experts. In the contemporary mind-set, it is a discipline to be understood and implemented by common people.

On the whole, it has been a good and useful tool. Psychologists and their theories have helped us better understand ourselves and have given us motivation to improve. The danger, though, is that some people wish to make the tool a god. In a desperate attempt to glue together the pieces of their lives, they enshrine a certain theorist as messiah and pin their hope for wholeness on his message.

Psychology as an instrument is helpful; psychology as a religion promises far more than it can deliver. Paul Vitz, in his book *Psychology as Religion*, declared that psychology is indeed a religion in our country, and a destructive one:

> Psychology has become a religion, in particular, a form of secular humanism based on worship of the self. . . . Psychology as religion has for years been destroying individuals, families, and communities. But for the first time the destructive logic of this

secular religion is beginning to be understood, and as more and more people discover the emptiness of self-worship, Christianity is presented with a major historical opportunity to provide meaning and life.[1]

Those strong words, from the pen of a trained psychologist, ought to make us look again at the role psychology should play in our society. They also ought to remind followers of Christ that no human system can take the place of God's design for wholeness.

Modern psychology's tendency is for us to turn all of our attention to our "selves." Yes, self-awareness is necessary, but being overly preoccupied with self is a sure way to wind up both selfish and depressed. When psychology becomes our hope for salvation, we become sophisticated introverts gazing at our own psyches, and God and people are almost forgotten. Too much modern psychology preaches the motto, "To find your life you must go looking for it," rather than Jesus' idea that we find our lives by losing them. As Vitz wrote:

> It should be obvious—though it has apparently not been so to many—that the relentless and single-minded search for and glorification of the self is at direct cross-purposes with the Christian injunction to *lose* the self. Certainly Jesus Christ neither lived nor advocated a life that would qualify by today's standards as "self-actualized." For the Christian the self is the problem, not the potential paradise.[2]

Augustine, Luther, and other Christian leaders in the past have declared that the essence of sin is "man turned in upon himself." It is the insistence of contemporary psychology that "we turn in upon ourselves" that finally makes it a bogus gospel. For if we are created in the image of the Divine Maker, and if we are basically spiritual beings, psychology's plea that we be reconciled to our "selves" is incomplete. Because we are created in God's image as basically spiritual beings, we must also be reconciled to

God, and any scheme that leaves the God question unanswered is not the path to real salvation.

Salvation Through Success

The late Carlyle Marney used to speak of humanity's quest for "salvation by successing." That phrase carries with it the idea that humanity's wholeness is directly related to personal achievements. If a person can garner all five of the pieces of the "success pie," if a person can gain reputation and fame, and if a person can experience consistent pleasure, then it is assumed that one will be rescued from emptiness. He or she will "have it all together," to use our modern phrase for wholeness of life. Salvation, according to this false view, is a commodity that can be earned if a person is successful enough.

When we base our wholeness on our success, we will naturally do anything to be successful. We will dress a certain way, act a certain way, even smell a certain way if that's what it takes to be accepted. In a salvation-through-success society, people become the kind of human chameleons Erich Fromm once described:

> The aim of the marketing character is complete adaptation, so as to be desirable under all conditions of the personality market. The marketing character personalities do not even *have* egos (as people in the nineteenth century did) to hold onto, that belong to them, that do not change. For they constantly change their egos, according to the principle: "I am as you desire me."[3]

If salvation depends on success, and success depends on marketing one's character, let us all package ourselves attractively and sell ourselves to the highest bidder. For then, and only then, will we be "saved."

The problem with this view of wholeness, of course, is that

it makes our salvation a pawn of public opinion. Since our lives must be successful and since the people around us define success, we are at the mercy of others. The foundation for our lives becomes the shifting sand of popular acclaim, and we do not know who we are or how successful we are until we see our reflection in someone else's eyes.

Jesus' question, "For what will a man be profited, if he gains the whole world, and forfeits his soul?" (Matt. 16:26) is especially disturbing to anyone seeking "salvation by successing." It suggests that the spiritual dimension of people is crucial and that money, fame, power, and popularity are not ultimate values after all. That one piercing question makes us look again at what salvation is and what real success involves.

On several occasions, Jesus indicated that the poor are peculiarly blessed. Most of us, upon reading that truth, probably pray that God will spare us that blessing! If we must be poor to be blessed, we'll gladly skip God's favor! But the poor are peculiarly blessed because they are not as prone to believe they can have salvation through success. They cannot depend upon achievement and acclaim for salvation. The poor are blessed because they are dependent and desperate. In their dependency and desperation, they are prime candidates for the kingdom Christ came to establish.

Even a quick glance around our society indicates that many now believe they *will* find their souls as soon as they gain the whole world. They have embarked on frantic journeys toward the port of success because they believe they will find wholeness of life and lasting contentment once they arrive there.

If the Bible is anywhere near the truth, and I believe it is, those voyagers are moving in the wrong direction, and, even if they do one day find "success," they will never find the salvation they so earnestly seek.

Salvation Through Sincerity

The third way many moderns seek salvation is through sincerity. The credo of the "sincerists" goes like this: It doesn't matter much what you believe as long as your intentions are right. Be nice, do good deeds, pay your taxes, and go to church. If your good deeds outnumber your bad ones, you will be happy and you will be whole, both now and forevermore.

Calvin Miller took these sincerists to task when he wrote:

> Probably the most popular alternative to the "way of the cross" is the sincerity cult. To the devotees of this cult, doctrine is unimportant. All that matters is sincerity. Even the aborigine with his neck ringed in tiger teeth, if faithful to his amulet, will reach God as surely as the apostle Paul. Sincerity and salvation are synonyms. Ignoring the consideration that people can be sincerely wrong, the sincerist says, "I may, in truth, be wrong but Infinite Love will consider my sincerity." Such self-styled religion is disgusting.[4]

Sincerity salvation ignores content and places a premium on intention and intensity. According to this line of thought, if a person's intentions are good and if that person pursues goodness with intense fervor, then he or she is on the road to life abundant and life eternal. It *is* an attractive philosophy simply because it contains so much truth. Intentions *are* important. Intensity *is* a virtue, and goodness *is* the mark of a godly person. Much in this "good" theory mirrors the biblical material on love and kindness.

However, from the Bible's point of view, sincerity salvation has one tragic flaw: it fails to consider the cross. If people could be sincere enough, good enough, or moral enough, Jesus could have avoided the anguish experienced at the cross. As Miller wrote:

> If there had been any other way for men to be saved, there would never have been a Calvary. Our Lord endured the ugliness of it all, not so that men might have some alternate route of redemption,

but because there was no other way. Had there been some less expensive way, He would never have gone back to the Father with scarred hands. Nor would He ever have suffered a naked death before His dear, earthly mother. If there had been any other approach to God, He would have shouted the command to angelic legions, waiting at rapt attention for the call to deliver Him.[5]

Salvation through sincerity is a hope widely held in our day. But because people can be sincerely wrong and because it fails to recognize the cross, salvation through sincerity only leaves one sincerely lost.

Salvation: God's Way

The biblical way to salvation is not through psychology, success, or sincerity; it is through the Savior, Jesus Christ:

I am the way, and the truth, and the life; no one comes to the Father, but through Me (John 14:6).

And there is salvation in no one else; for there is no other name under heaven that has been given among men, by which we must be saved (Acts 4:12).

I came that they might have life, and might have it abundantly (John 10:10).

Through Christ's cross and resurrection, the biblical writers found a dynamic that could put together again the pieces of their lives. In him, they found life abundant on earth and the promise of life eternal tomorrow. Through Christ, they found a way to escape the meaningless humdrum of trivial existence.

In the Book of Romans, Paul tried to verbalize what Christ and his cross had meant to him. He described the implications of the life, death, and resurrection of Christ for all humankind and, in doing so, gave depth to the declaration, "Jesus saves." In Paul's eyes, Jesus saves because:

He shows us the meaning of love and guarantees God's care for us (Rom. 5:8; 8:38-39).

He enables us to relax and have peace because he has justified us with God (Rom. 5:1).

He sets us free from bondage to sin and self-centeredness (Rom. 6:6-7; 8:1-2).

He gives us hope that we, too, can overcome seeming defeat and tragedy (Rom. 5:2-5).

He provides us the possibility to change and to become new people (Rom. 6:4).

He takes the sting out of death and translates despair into eternal life (Rom. 5:20-21; 6:23).

When Paul looked back at Jesus' life, death, and resurrection, he saw not merely historical events but far-reaching implications that could totally convert a person's life. In Christ, Paul saw love, peace, freedom, hope, change, and eternal life. In a word, he saw salvation: "For I am not ashamed of the gospel, for it is the power of God for salvation to every one who believes" (Rom. 1:16).

The biblical message concerning salvation has not changed. In spite of sophistication and technological advance, people will find salvation only through the Savior. A person may be a keen student of the psychological trends and theories of the day; a person may become rich, famous, and successful by every standard the world has; and a person can be sincere in morals and convictions, but if a person has not personally received Christ and his gifts, that person will never be whole.

In his book, *Fully Human, Fully Alive*, John Powell listed five steps to fullness of life: "(1) to *accept* oneself (2) to *be* oneself (3) to *forget* oneself in loving (4) to *believe* (5) to *belong*".[6] If those are really necessary components of the abundant life, it is apparent why Christ is the key to real living. He offers to provide all five of these needs in a person's life if only given the opportunity.

To Accept Oneself

Transactional Analysis declares, "I'm OK, you're OK." The gospel begs to differ. It offers instead a view of humanity that cries out, "I'm not OK, and you're not OK. But because of Christ, that's OK." In the biblical view, a person is OK because of what Jesus has done for humanity. Self-acceptance is a natural part of the Christians' birthright because Christ has accepted them and, thus, they can accept themselves. In the death of Christ, every person can see his or her own intrinsic worth. Imagine the wonder of it all: "God demonstrates His own love toward us, in that while we were yet sinners, Christ died for us" (Rom. 5:8). If that statement won't enable us to accept ourselves, nothing in the world will! And always undergirding a Christian's self-concept is grace. Even when the Christian does stumble, grace lends a steadying hand. Even when the Christian grows discouraged, grace whispers words of love and acceptance. Grace, that unmerited favor of the Father, is always present to buoy our spirits and remind us we are sons and daughters of the King. An understanding of Christ's death and the grace it purchased makes self-acceptance a continual reality for the true believer.

To Be Oneself

Having accepted oneself—sins, personality flaws, and all— one is then better able to be oneself. It is a lifelong adventure trying to be that peculiar and special person God wants us to be. My mind applauds the awe of each individual's uniqueness and the excitement of the quest to live that unique life. Regrettably, I have occasionally followed Peter's timid path and denied my own identity for a few fleeting moments of crowd approval. I know I'm not always as true to myself and my uniqueness as I should be.

But because of my commitment to Christ, I have more confidence to be myself, to dare to be the person I feel God has made me to be, to put on public display *my* beliefs, *my* feelings, *my* personality. And where else can I find a model like Jesus? What other system can give me such a living symbol of integrity? Even the prospect of a horrid death could not make Jesus deny himself. He was determined to be the man he was made to be, taking the journey he was made to take. That encourages me to be myself and to strike out on the journey I sense God wants me to travel.

To Forget Oneself in Loving

Why, that is the very core of Christianity! That's what Christ is all about! Anyone who takes seriously Christ's command, "Follow me," will have to move along the path of selfless love. In Christ, we forget ourselves in loving. We find our lives by losing them. We have crucifixion so someone else can have resurrection. We follow the One who gave his life so others could live.

To Believe

Every person needs a reason to live and a reason to die. Without a mission, a cause, a faith to believe in, human personality withers into pale lifelessness. Christ gives us reason to believe. He offers us, not a philosophical system to accept or reject, but an opportunity to follow him, to assume the same priorities he has, to reorient our lives around him. The word *religion* literally means "to bind together," and Christ offers us religion at its best. He can bind our tattered lives together and provide us that all-important reason to live and reason to die.

To Belong

Every person needs community. "It is not good for the man to be alone," (Gen. 2:18) God remarked at Eden. People have always flourished when they "belong" somewhere, when they can give love to and receive love from other humans. Jesus offers us community in his church. When that community rightly fulfills its role, it is a warm, honest group where the healing of emotional wounds occurs. Who comes when I am sick? Who stands with me when my knees quiver? Who laughs at my joys and cries at my sorrows? Who prods me into self-examination and repentance? When it is really fulfilling its purpose, my church does. It is the one organism where people like me can really belong.

What Paul found to be true and expressed to the Roman Christians, I have also verified: Jesus Christ meets the most pressing needs of human beings. Whether those needs are expressed in Pauline terminology (love, peace, freedom, and so forth) or the five modern phrases of John Powell, the truth is the same. Christ is our only hope for salvation.

Paul knew, even in his day, that his message of salvation through Christ would not be well-received. To the Jews, he wrote, his message would be a stumbling block. To the Gentiles, salvation through a Jewish Savior would sound like sheer folly. But Paul had already traveled the road of worldly wisdom and had found it to be a dead-end street. He would stake his life on "the foolishness of the cross" and the One who died there.

Our world likewise will seek better ways to find fullness of life. Psychology will be a religion for some. Success will lure others into its fold. And some will build their hopes for today and tomorrow on their own sincerity. But some will dare to believe that Christ is still "'the way, and the truth, and the life,'" (John 14:6) and, with Paul, will declare, "We are fools for Christ's sake" (1 Cor. 4:10). Those "fools" will be those rescued from emptiness today and then delivered into the presence of God himself tomorrow.

Notes

1. Paul C. Vitz, *Psychology as Religion: The Cult of Self-Worship* (Grand Rapids: William B. Eerdmans Publishing Co., 1977), pp. 9,10.

2. Ibid, p. 91.

3. Erich Fromm, *To Have or to Be?* (New York: Harper and Row, 1976), p. 148.

4. Calvin Miller, *Once Upon a Tree* (Grand Rapids: Baker Book House, 1967), p. 40.

5. Ibid, p. 41.

6. John Powell, *Fully Human, Fully Alive* (Niles, Illinois: Argus Communications, 1976), p. 23.

7

Time:

The Right Now or the Heavenly Hope?

Theological pendulums swing to extremes. Let one generation caricature God as an austere tyrant, and the next generation might fluctuate to the opposite position and picture God as "Good Buddy." Let one generation see the Bible as directly penned by the Heavenly Author, and the next might react by claiming that God's part in inspiration was small. Whenever the pendulum swings too far in one direction, look for the reactors to push it too far in the other direction.

For a long while, the pendulum in evangelical Christianity swung toward eternity. Sermons on the splendor of heaven and the horrors of hell were preached with regularity forty or fifty years ago. People were urged to accept Christ primarily because their eternity was at stake. Critics of the "eternity emphasis" called this "pie-in-the-sky-by-and-by" preaching and criticized it for its omission of the present dimension of salvation. And eventually the pendulum started to swing toward the rewards and responsibilities of Christians *today*. Life *before* death, instead of life *after* death, became the focal point of sermons and books on the Christian faith.

It was a needed movement, simply because a decision to follow Christ does have implications for today. A commitment to Christ is never an escape from reality. It is never a pious pining for the hereafter. It is a decision to let Christ bless us and use us in the here and now.

But now we must ask ourselves if, in our desire to right the distortions of the previous generation, we might have pushed the pendulum too far in the other direction. In our justifiable desire to emphasize that Christ makes a difference before we die, have we failed to say we believe he also makes a difference *after* we die? In emphasizing abundant life, have we forgotten eternal life? And in proclaiming the present dimension of our relationship with Christ, have we inadvertently neglected the eternal one?

The modern world, with its hunger for instant answers and immediate gratification, would have us speak more about today than tomorrow. Gore Vidal writes of "today's passion for the immediate and the casual," and that passion of which he speaks gravitates against either belief or interest in eternal life. We are a nation of thirty-second commercials and thirty-minute dramas. Get the sales pitch to us quickly, and we might buy. Introduce the characters, create the plot, and resolve the conflict in thirty minutes, or you won't sustain our interest. What is done must be done quickly and efficiently because we're all busy and life is short. Talk of what will happen beyond the grave is, for the "now generation," both boring and speculative.

Besides, a belief in life beyond the grave is not too chic these days. After all, the Russian cosmonaut ventured into the heavens a number of years back and reported no sign of Deity anywhere. And we now know that the universe is not the three-storied scheme which was the prevalent view centuries ago. Some skeptics assert that science has seemingly moved us beyond the biblical material on eternal destiny.

In a desire to be both credible and appealing to our world, our tendency as Christians is to downplay eternity. Who wants to appear naive to friends? Who wants to play the fool needlessly? Who wants to speak of eternal destiny when the real interest of humanity seems to be inflation and the Super Bowl?

Before we abandon our message of eternity, we would do well to take stock of what we lose when we focus only on "the now." We should realize that much is at stake on the biblical declarations about eternal life. On the accuracy of those biblical passages concerning the eternal dimension hang the truthfulness of our Bible, the significance of our actions, the reality of our hope, and the reason for our peace. Without the heavenly hope, we are destitute.

The Truthfulness of Our Bible

Over and over, the biblical writers speak of eternal life. If we do not focus on the eternal dimension of our faith, we will have to disregard much of the New Testament, for it is brimming with talk of eternity. A brief sampling looks like this:

Jesus: " 'In My Father's house are many dwelling places; if it were not so, I would have told you; for I go to prepare a place for you' " (John 14:2).

"These will go away into eternal punishment, but the righteous into eternal life' " (Matt. 25:46).

" 'Whoever believes in Him should not perish, but have eternal life' " (John 3:16).

Paul: "For this perishable must put on the imperishable, and this mortal must put on immortality" (1 Cor. 15:53).

"For the wages of sin is death, but the free gift of God is eternal life in Christ Jesus our Lord" (Rom. 6:23).

John: "These things I have written to you who believe in the name of the Son of God, in order that you may know that you have eternal life" (1 John 5:13).

"He shall wipe away every tear from their eyes; and there shall no longer be any mourning, or crying, or pain; the first things have passed away" (Rev. 21:4).

Peter: "His great mercy has caused . . . to obtain an
          inheritance which is imperishable and undefiled
          and will not fade away, reserved in heaven for you"
          (1 Pet. 1:4).

Over forty times in the New Testament, the word *eternal* is
used, indicating the forward look and future hope of the early
saints. Images are used to depict heaven and hell. The imagery of
flames and torment, golden streets and crystal rivers describes real
conditions. The inescapable conclusion an honest person must
live with is that eternal life is a biblical concept and that Jesus
Christ holds the key to one's eternal destiny.

It behooves the Christian to refrain from trying to describe
the furniture of heaven or the exact temperature of hell. We do
not know everything about the life to come and should not act
like we do. But I also agree with the apostle Paul, "If we have
only hoped in Christ in this life, we are of all men most to be
pitied" (1 Cor. 15:19). Though we do not know everything about
eternity, we have pinned our hopes on Christ and trust that he
can, indeed, transport us safely to the other side.

Because the New Testament is so adamant in its claims for
eternal life, we downplay eternity only at the risk of downplaying
much of the written Word. We cannot stop speaking of the
heavenly hope simply because our society no longer finds such
talk palatable, and we cannot "doctor" the Bible to make it fit the
popular mind-set. We must continue to uphold the eternal
dimension of our faith.

The Significance of Our Actions

Without the promise of eternal life, our actions lose much of
their significance. As Henry Sloane Coffin once wrote:

It might be supposed that those who consider our earthly years all
that we possess would prize their every moment more highly than

those who fancy that unending aeons lie before them. But that is
not the case. When once a man is convinced that seventy or eighty
years at the outside are all that will ever be his in the ongoings of
the universe, they seem so trivial in comparison with the vast
sweep of the centuries, that it matters little what he does with
himself in them. Whenever men have said, "Tomorrow we die,"
they have played fast and loose with today.[1]

The old Epicurean idea of eating and drinking and being
merry is predicated upon the fact that tomorrow we're all going to
die. Since nothing has eternal significance, why not grab all the
gusto we can get today? Why not eat, drink, and be merry if
tomorrow our lives will be snuffed out like used-up candles?

The biblical vantage point is that our actions today are
important because they impinge upon tomorrow. In the Bible,
the temporal affects the eternal and is, therefore, of great
consequence. Because of the hope of life after death, one's vocation
is not just necessary labor to make money; it is a response to the
divine plan and a preparation for further service in eternity.
Because of the eternal dimension, a friendship is not merely a
passing relationship that will be extinguished by the tomb; it is a
relationship that can last and grow forever. Because of eternity,
family life is not an obligation to be discharged or even a pleasant
situation that ends all too quickly; it is a joyful celebration of
relationships on earth that may be continued in heaven. Because
of the hope of eternal life, building character is not a futile
endeavor that ends at the grave; it is a wise investment that will
reap everlasting dividends. All of these things gain meaning when
we believe in eternal life and, without eternity, our lives have only
minor consequence. If all that we are and believe and have discovered
is destroyed at death, life is both futile and empty.

Jesus could relate to people as he did because he believed his
actions had eternal consequence. He could bear the anxiety of
Gethsemane because he knew God could redeem that anxiety in

eternity. Jesus could hang from the cross because he trusted that death would not put an end to who he was and what he had done. He could walk out of the tomb on resurrection Sunday because he knew he had a life with his Father in front of him. Jesus could act with love, integrity, and courage in his present because he believed in his future.

When we downplay the Bible's promises concerning eternal life, we lose some of our motivation to live *today*. Our actions then have little significance, and our lives have little meaning.

The Reality of Our Hope

"But now abide faith, hope, love, these three; but the greatest of these is love" (1 Cor. 13:13). Love may be the greatest of the abiding virtues, but don't ever shortchange faith and hope. Without faith, human beings become self-sufficient machines or scared, pitiful animals. Without hope, humans become angry cynics or somber fatalists.

Peggy Lee's song of several years ago "Is That All There Is?" captures the plight of the person without hope. After describing both ecstatic experiences and agonizing ones, the song heaves a disappointed sigh about everything and asks, "Is that all there is to life?" Like the preacher in Ecclesiastes, the song arrives at the conclusion that "all is vanity." And much in current philosophy and psychology echoes a mournful "amen."

The futility of life is vividly captured in a phrase from one of John Masefield's poems. A widowed mother watches as her son is led to the gallows for a crime he committed. As the rope does its horrible work, the grief-stricken mother begins to sob; and those nearby hear her mumble something about "broken things too broke to mend." That terrible phrase describes the feelings many people secretly have. Because of the death or the divorce or the financial disaster, they see life as "too broke to mend" and join the ever-growing chorus singing the "all-is-vanity" song (Eccl. 12:8).

But the Bible encourages us to hope, even when suffering and setback are our companions. As Paul wrote, that hope is not only in this life but also in the one yet to come. The Bible declares that death itself died on Easter Sunday morning. From the biblical perspective, death is a paper tiger that, though terrifying in appearance, has no real power to destroy the man or woman in Christ. Because even the ultimate enemy, death, has been revealed as a passageway to God for the Christian, the biblical admonition over and over is to hope:

"We exult in hope of the glory of God" (Rom. 5:2).

"Rejoicing in hope" (Rom. 12:12).

"Through perseverance and the encouragement of the Scriptures we might have hope" (Rom. 15:4).

"The hope laid up for you in heaven" (Col. 1:5).

"That you may not grieve, as do the rest who have no hope." (1 Thess. 4:13).

"To realize the full assurance of hope until the end" (Heb. 6:11).

"Has caused us to be born again to a living hope through the resurrection of Jesus Christ from the dead" (1 Pet. 1:3).

Take away the promise of eternal life and the Christian might as well pitch in with the "all-is-vanity" chorale. Christian hope is built upon the promise of empowered life *before* death and resurrection life *after* death. Because of that two-pronged hope, it is the Christian's conviction that nothing in life, or in death, is "too broke to mend." "This hope we have as an anchor of the soul, a hope both sure and steadfast" (Heb. 6:19).

The Reason for Our Peace

One of my fantasies is to escape someday to the country, raise a few cows, write a few books, entertain a few friends, and generally get away from the hectic pace of urban life. Occasionally, I will pick up a book by some author who has opted for a simple, rustic existence, and I become green with envy. It would be great to walk in the woods, fish for days without feeling guilty, and take some long afternoon naps.

Yet, I secretly fear that the fulfillment of that fantasy would be a disappointment to me. I'm afraid my sojourn in the country would turn out to be disillusioning. I say that because in the early seventies I had the opportunity to spend a summer in the country. I was a newlywed seminary student and the pastor of a country church in central Texas. We decided to spend the summer "on the field."

The setting was perfect: we lived in a new mobile home, did a bit of gardening, had hours of free time, and even had a neighbor's cows grazing contentedly in the field behind us. The people were gracious and friendly and accepted us gladly as part of the community. But, surprisingly, we quickly grew apprehensive in our relaxed environment. By the end of the summer, we couldn't wait to reenter seminary and rejoin the rat race! All that freedom and quiet in seclusion created a restlessness in me. But my memory is not too good sometimes, and I still fantasize about the peace and joy of a life in the wilderness.

If nothing else, though, my summer in the country of central Texas taught me, or reminded me, that peace is not found in a particular place. "The peace that passes all understanding" of which Paul spoke is not dependent upon place or circumstance. It is an inner direction and meaning that enables a person to be content wherever he or she might be: "for I have learned to be content in whatever circumstances I am" (Phil. 4:11). Peace can be found in Houston, as well as in the backwoods. It can be found in disappointment, as well as in triumph. Peace is a gift of God to those who have entrusted themselves unreservedly into his care.

And the hope of eternity is a factor in this peace. The

promise of eternal life to all who know Christ enables a person to relax, to slow down, to be at peace in this world. If there is a loving God and if he has provided an eternity for those who trust him, much of the anxiety of being human is relieved. I affirm the Christian belief that death has been defeated, relationships can be truly lasting, dreams can be eventually fulfilled, character can finally be perfected, and ultimate truth can be discovered. But apart from the hope of eternity, life is marked by a natural tension and pressure. Here and now death does destroy, relationships are fleeting, dreams are illusory, character will always be imperfect, and the lack of final truth is frustrating. The person without the hope of eternity is destined for anxiety. Life for the hopeless is a mad dash to see how much can be accumulated before time runs out.

For the ones who have pinned their lives on the truth of the Bible, however, peace and relaxation may reign supreme. In the words of the writer of Hebrews, we who have believed have "entered into God's rest." There is no need to rush through life as if there is no tomorrow. There is no need to see time as an enemy. Our lives are in the hands of the eternal God, who miraculously loves us as we are and has redeemed us through Christ. Like the birds of the air and the lilies of the field, we can look to him for life. And, in that looking, we can have peace.

Because so much of our faith is based upon the eternal dimension, we must make sure that it has a place in our life philosophies and in our preaching and teaching. We who would conform to the teachings of the Bible will hold onto the eternal dimension because we are destitute without it.

Our world wants to see God now, but we can offer only faith now and realized proof tomorrow. Our world wants instant gratification, but we can only answer that much of life is mystery and that some rewards will have to wait for eternity. Our world wants gimmicks, miracles, and easy answers, but we can tell only of Jesus and his love and then encourage people to follow him. Our world wants the proof found in test tubes and computers, but we can offer only the hope of an unseen eternity with an unseen God.

Those "onlys" are enough. If our world will not "buy" our message, we must not change it to make it look and sound more "modern." That only cheapens our message and destroys our uniqueness. We must, rather, cast our lives on the truth of the Bible and proclaim it unashamedly. We must also cling to the hope of eternal life and trust that the God who loves us now will someday call us to him.

Armed with that hope, who or what can possibly defeat us?

Note

1. Henry Sloane Coffin, "Facing Extinction" in *20 Centuries of Great Preaching*, Volume VIII (Waco: Word Books, 1971), p. 297.

8
Influence:
Noninterference or Redemptive Light?

My "witnessing button" made me miserable for weeks. The yellow button had a red maze on it and was to be displayed on a shirt or coat to attract interest. When some curious inquirer asked about the button, the wearer then had the green light to explain that Jesus Christ was the way out of the maze of life. My problem was simple: I was afraid to wear my button.

It glared at me from my jewelry box for much of my freshman year at college. Everytime I reached for a tie tack the button would sneer at me and remind me what a fearful and pitiful Christian I was. Finally, I reached a compromise that eased the guilt which was building up within me. I took the witnessing button out of the jewelry box, pinned it on my shirt, and then put a jacket over it! Then I could comfort myself with the knowledge that I had the nerve to wear the button and be assured, at the same time, no one would ever have enough of a peek to ask me about it. I wore my witnessing button for days and never had to tell anyone how Jesus had delivered me from life's maze.

That incident is symbolic of my nearly lifelong quest to influence people for Christ. On the one hand, I have felt a need, a compulsion, a desire to tell others about Christ. On the other hand, I have struggled with shyness and inadequacy and haven't done as much verbal witnessing as I would have liked. Part of me has always wanted to don a witnessing button, but another part of my makeup has always suggested I put a jacket over it.

My feelings, I have now discovered, are common. Many Christians feel the same tension I have felt. They want to be personal evangelists but don't feel confident or capable enough, and the result is guilt and feelings of failure. This chapter is directed to all such guilt-ridden strugglers with the hope that some motivation and information can be provided.

The Bible gives us a definite mandate to tell others of Christ. If we have studied the Bible at all, we recognize that evangelism is not just the calling of preachers and professionals. Every person who follows Jesus Christ is given a summons to go and bear the good news. The Great Commission enjoins us to go into all the world. Acts 1:8 tells us to be witnesses in Jerusalem, Judea, Samaria, and unto the uttermost part of the earth. In the Sermon on the Mount, Jesus called his followers "the salt of the earth" (Matt. 5:13) and "the light of the world" (Matt. 5:14), and both salt and light conjure up images of penetration and change. Paul observed that God has committed to us the word of reconciliation and that we are ambassadors for Christ (see 2 Cor. 5:18-20). Whether the Bible speaks of being witnesses, salt, light, reconcilers, or ambassadors, the message is the same: the Christian is supposed to exert influence for Jesus Christ.

That message runs head-on into a popular mood that deplores salesmanship and pressure of any kind. Our world has been so bombarded with revolutionary new products, investment opportunities, and self-help techniques that it now wants to be left mercifully alone. In a media-oriented society, where billboards sparkle, radios blare, and telephones jangle, seclusion is a precious state of being. The plea of modern people is aptly expressed in the phrase from a country song of a few years ago— "just leave this long-haired country boy alone." We may not all be long-haired country boys, but most of us *would* like to be left alone. "I'll do it my way," modern people say. "Different strokes for different folks," "What turns you on may not turn me on," and other recent expressions capture our society's desire for independence and freedom from outside pressure.

So, the modern Christian is stuck squarely between the proverbial rock and hard place. On one side is a gospel that challenges one to be an influence, a persuader, for Christ. On the other side is a world that resents obvious attempts at influence, a world already "turned off" by too much persuasion. What is the stuck-in-the middle follower of Christ to do?

Well, the Christian can do one of three things. First, one can choose to become another blaring voice in the din of noise trying to sway modern people. One can venture where angels fear to tread and say one's piece as loud and aggressively as the rest. This approach to evangelism emphasizes boldness at the expense of sensitivity. The goal is to put the message across and to obtain decisions; sometimes this goal is reached and people find Christ. Sometimes, however, this approach lowers the evangelist to the level of the street-hawker and makes the gospel sound like a new fad or the latest labor-saving gimmick. When that happens, the cause of Christ suffers, for searching people are repulsed by "gadget" religion and loud, but cheap, answers.

Second, one can choose to be quiet and say nothing about Christ. This approach to evangelism emphasizes sensitivity at the expense of boldness. The "silent witness" is the sensitive soul who does not want to appear judgmental or dogmatic. That kind of witness wants to be affirming and accepting and therefore is reluctant to suggest that his/her friend needs Christ. It is one of the great tragedies of modern Christendom that these sensitive, caring people, who would make the best Christian persuaders, have voted for silence.

Third, the stuck-in-the-middle follower of Christ can choose the path of sensitive boldness. One can endeavor to walk that narrow line between brash boldness and silent sensitivity, and somehow capture the best of both. The third approach will be

most effective in introducing others to Christ and must become
our aim. The loud, dogmatic witnesses must pray for love and the
capacity to feel with others. The quiet, sincere witnesses must
pray for opportunities to tell of Christ and then be more
aggressive in seizing those opportunities.

For years, I have been piecing together a mental scrapbook
on personally influencing others for Christ. Eight ideas now have
a prominent place in that scrapbook. I detail them for you with
the hope that they will help you be both sensitive and bold in
your own witnessing for Christ.

Check Your Spiritual Temperature

Witnessing for Christ has more to do with who you are than
with what you do. The key to Christian influence is not a certain
technique or program, but a distinctive commitment that gives
direction, enthusiasm, and support to your life. *Being* precedes
doing, and any approach to personal witnessing which majors on
method has a faulty premise. The place to begin is with character
and spiritual fervor.

The prerequisite to Christian influence is a living relationship with Christ. Without that life-enriching relationship, all of
the methods and techniques one might employ in evangelism are
useless. The basic questions we must ask ourselves are simple and
direct: *Do I have a personal relationship with Christ? Is that
relationship growing and maturing? Am I enthusiastic about the
Christian life? Does it give me a feeling of wonder about God and the life
he has given me? Can I stand on my own experience and find it solid? Do
I want others to find what I have found in Christ?* The answers to
those kinds of questions provide the basis for effective Christian
persuasion. If the answers are affirmative and if we are captivated
by Jesus Christ, we have something far more vital to "the stuff" of
witnessing than any scheme or program. We have a life that
testifies to the truth of our gospel.

Until we are secure in our own spiritual pilgrimage and excited about it, we will have little motivation to tell others about our Lord. Perhaps we will occasionally hear a sermon that will make us feel guilty and motivate us to witness. Or we might read a book on personal evangelism which will set us on a temporary witnessing binge. But to be consistent, faithful witnesses, we must have a conviction that Christ makes a daily difference in our lives. Without that conviction, apathy about evangelism will eventually overtake us.

There are three primary reasons why people fail to influence others for Christ. One reason is a feeling of inadequacy. Many people will never speak of spiritual things because they feel they don't know enough about the Bible or about how to converse with people. They feel incompetent and so leave evangelism to the preachers and professionals.

A second reason Christians don't witness is fear. Who wants to run the risk of rejection? Who wants to look like a religious fanatic? Who wants to speak of spiritual things in a world that discourages "religious talk"? Who wants to bare his soul to a friend and then receive apathy or hostility in return? Fear of these things inhibits most of us and makes us reluctant to speak of our walk with Christ.

The third deterrent to witnessing is spiritual apathy, and I believe it is the biggest deterrent of all. To put it bluntly, most Christians never evangelize because Jesus Christ is not that important to them! They want to go to church occasionally and even contribute when the offering plate is passed. They want their children to be in church; they want them to know of Jesus, the Ten Commandments, and the good Samaritan. But these people are not ready for the demanding Jesus of the New Testament and his radical teachings. They are not prepared for "the [road] less traveled by," the road to dedicated discipleship, and thus they never experience the purpose and enthusiasm that could be theirs.

Though it hurts to admit it, the one overriding deterrent to our evangelism is our apathy. People who have never been disturbed and blessed in their own journeys with Christ will always lack motivation to tell others about him.

Therefore, the only stable foundation for personal evangelism is built of conviction and enthusiasm. Always, before we look at "what we do," we must scrutinize "who we are." Obviously, we are sinners with personal hang-ups, inadequacies, fears, and limitations. But is Christ Lord of our lives? Are we excited about serving him? Have we tested him in the crucible of our own experiences and found him trustworthy? Can we say with the apostle, "For to me, to live is Christ"? (Phil. 1:21).

Before we pass out tracts or ring doorbells or attend another evangelism seminar, let's take our spiritual temperature. For the plain truth is this: lukewarm saints simply cannot light a fire.

Drop Some Theological Anchors

A boat on the seas without an anchor is destined to drift if it loses power. Followers of Christ without some specific convictions are destined to drift too. Without some definite theological anchors, Christians are moored only to emotion or circumstance, and those are uncertain docks at best. Without some definite theological anchors, Christians will also find it hard to become motivated to witness.

Three "anchors" are indispensable to a personal theology of evangelism. Those anchors are (1) people have a desperate need, (2) Jesus Christ meets that need, and (3) God uses people as his ambassadors. If any one of these three ingredients is missing, we will never be motivated to tell others about Christ.

People's most pressing need, simply put, is God. People never have been able to live by bread alone. We must have God. And if we can't find the true one, we will invent one of our own. Centuries ago, Augustine spoke of a yearning in humanity that could only be satisfied by a relationship with God. Today, as always, people are trying to satisfy that yearning with money, houses, vacations, sex, and power. But even with the acquisition of these things, the yearning remains and the frustration level rises. Apart from God, people are truly lost, groping, and disillusioned. We have a need for direction, love, hope, and eternal life that can be met only by our Creator. If that is not true, if people can fare as well without God as with him, then Christian witnesses are only religious propagandists selling false merchandise. If it *is* true—and I believe it is—and people are destitute apart from God, then witnesses are the bearers of the world's best news. Their vocation is an urgent one.

The Bible asserts that Jesus Christ supplies that all-important oneness with the Father. "God was in Christ reconciling the world to Himself" (2 Cor. 5:19). Jesus himself said, "No one comes to the Father, but through Me" (John 14:6). The mediator between God and humanity is Jesus, born in Bethlehem, crucified at Calvary, and resurrected to live in the hearts of people. If this Jesus were a fake messiah or if he were just one route to God among many, there should be no real effort to introduce him to others. But this Jesus is the Christ, the true Messiah, and the one Savior of the world. He ought to be proclaimed to all people everywhere.

The Bible also asserts that God has entrusted this good news to people. Rather than dazzle people with his splendor or thunder divine edicts from the heavens, God has mysteriously chosen to work through people who have experienced the truth of his Son. He has chosen to put the treasure of his love into marred, earthen vessels. If God did "his thing" without people, evangelism would be a futile endeavor. But God uses people as ambassadors of his love, so influencing others for Christ is one's most pressing work.

If people have no need, we would be foolish to invent one. If Christ were not the one Savior, we would be mistakenly narrow-minded. And if God didn't use people in his plan of redemption, we would be getting in his way when we try to evangelize. However, we believe these three ideas are true: people do have a need, Christ meets that need, and Christians are called to cooperate with God. If we anchor our lives in these truths, we will find it necessary to discover a personal style of witnessing that will enable us to be effective persuaders for Christ.

Start at Jerusalem

Jesus commanded his followers to begin their witnessing activity where they were, in Jerusalem. The best place to be persuaders for Christ is where we are, with people we know. If we cannot display our Christian commitment to our family, friends, classmates, or job associates, we have little reason to dream of being dynamic evangelists in a faraway land. Evangelism must always begin close to home.

Our witness for our Lord must start at our own Jerusalem simply because that is where we are and also because that is where we will be most effective. With people who know and respect us, we will have the best results in our witnessing. Street-corner proclamation and random knocking on doors may yield some Christian decisions, but most will come in the context of personal relationships. Win Arn's survey of eight thousand lay people has shown that 70 to 90 percent of the people who join a particular church do so because friends or relatives attend that church. I believe people come to accept Jesus as Lord primarily because of friends or relatives too. When trust, respect, and mutuality have been established, we have the best forum for the message that has transformed our lives.

The reason relationships are so important to evangelism can be summed up in one word: credibility. When people see us as real people, as ordinary humans who like baseball or stamp collecting or ballet or needlework, we establish a certain trust-worthiness. We are not fanatics or lunatics or naive simpletons; we are ordinary people who have pledged our allegiance to Jesus. In the context of relationships, we become believable people with a believable message.

In the past two weeks, I have been approached from several directions by people wanting to sell me on something. A young man called and told me he had a way to save me quite a bit of money (he was in insurance, I believe). Another young man knocked on my door and wanted to revolutionize my life with his vacuum cleaner. A certain charity wrote to inform me that the survival of many children depended on my generous contribution. Another group wanted money to purchase Bibles for people in remote areas of the world. All four of these pleas were reasonable, but I turned a deaf ear to all of them.

Why? Because I had no relationship with the "evangelists," and there was no level of credibility established. But let a good friend tell me how to save tons of money, and I'll ask to hear more. Let a close comrade tell me how to save children's lives or provide Bibles for the spiritually hungry, and I'll probably make a generous contribution. Let a good friend testify that a certain vacuum cleaner has revolutionized his home, and I might even buy one of those. When a person I know and trust tells me something, it has a much greater impact than a phone call from a stranger or correspondence from afar.

The most effective personal witness is not the person who buttonholes people in the bus depot or passes out tracts to pedestrians. The most effective personal witness is the one who lives for Christ and tells of Christ in the everyday transactions of life. His witness is "personal" and is built upon a caring relationship. In and around his own Jerusalem, he makes it known that Jesus is Lord.

Be Flexible

A study of Jesus' dealings with people indicates he was both sensitive and flexible in his relationships. It appears he had no set plan or hard-and-fast method for pointing others to his Father. He met people where they were and varied his conversations according to a person's situation, need, and personality.

He spoke to Nicodemus, proud of his Jewish birth and heritage, of his need to be born again. He spoke to the woman at the well, who bounded from one sexual encounter to another, of her need for living water that could satisfy her thirst for meaning. He probed the rich, young ruler, proud of his status and wealth, at the point of his possessions and demanded that he change his priorities. To the self-righteous, legalistic Pharisees, Jesus spoke harsh words of accusation. When he met sick people craving health, he offered healing and spoke little of other things. He ate with the despised down-and-outers and identified with their hurts. He dealt with every person on an individual basis. Jesus was sensitive enough to see people's needs and bold enough to confront them with the news of a loving Father.

If we are going to be effective Christian persuaders, we, too, must be flexible in our relationships. We must learn to know people, to feel with them, and to identify with them. Some are angry at God because of past tragedy. Some are running from him out of guilt. Some feel too sophisticated for "naive" Christian doctrines. Some know absolutely nothing about the Bible, while others have grown up in the church and rebelled against it. Some people are wounded for life because of grief. Others are manipulative, cruel, and concerned only about self. But every person is a "thought of God" who needs to be approached with love and dignity. A Christlike flexibility is crucial to Christian witness.

There are two types of communication the witness can use in leading others to Christ, and sensitivity will determine when each type should be employed. Direct communication—an eyeball-to-eyeball encounter—is one type. In direct communication, the Christian presents the truth of his/her own experience or relates biblical passages that indicate how to have a relationship with the Father. Direct communication places the gospel openly before another person. The strengths of direct communication are many. It is straightforward. It provides a forum for give-and-take and honest discussion. It allows the witness to seek a response, and it allows the witness to express honest concern about the person's spiritual condition.

Indirect communication is the second type. In indirect communication, a person "overhears" the Christian message. When a person catches the enthusiasm and love of a particular church, he "overhears" something important about the Christian faith. When someone sees a flesh-and-blood example of Christianity or reads a thought-provoking book or attends a drama about the cross and resurrection, indirect communication takes place. This kind of communication has many benefits too. It emphasizes freedom and is not "pushy." It recognizes the privacy and sanctity of each individual. It builds credibility and provides a foundation for direct communication. It also creates curiosity and interest without intimidating confrontation.

Which type of communication should be used? Well, that varies from one situation to the next. The Christian must be flexible enough to employ the style that will best communicate the good news. Like our Lord, we modern-day disciples must learn to sense the needs and feelings of people, meet those people where they are, and then let them know that Christ can make an eternal difference in their lives.

Lean on the Spirit

If witnessing for Christ depends only on our efforts, we are in trouble. If our effectiveness depends on our knowledge, our relational skills, and our goodness, we might as well "throw in the towel." No one is smart enough, personable enough, or righteous enough to be a Christian persuader.

Thankfully, the Bible indicates that we are partners with God in redeeming his world. It emphasizes that God loves people, that he sent his Son to prove that love, and that he continues to draw people to him through the work of his Holy Spirit. Jesus promised his disciples that the Spirit would come to bear witness of him (John 15:26). Later John told the early church, "And it is the Spirit who bears witness, because the Spirit is the truth" (1 John 5:7). Christians are partners with the Spirit in the task of redemption and can therefore lean on him.

First, witnesses can lean on the Spirit for guidance. How do we know who is ready for the gospel? We trust that the Holy Spirit will lead us to those who are hungry for God. How do we know how to best communicate with a particular person? We pray for the Spirit's guidance and trust him to give us wisdom in our relationships. The Spirit leads us to people and gives us sensitivity, even though we may not often feel his presence.

Second, witnesses can lean on the Spirit for power. Jesus promised his disciples that they would receive power when the Spirit came upon them (Acts 1:8). If we have a relationship with God through Christ, that same power-inducing Spirit dwells within us. We do not witness in our own strength. We do not proclaim the good news in our own power. And we do not relate to others without a hidden Ally. The Spirit of Power lives within us to give us boldness and to transform even our fears and inadequacies into tools of reconciliation.

Third, witnesses lean on the Spirit for peace. Witnessing for Jesus Christ is a heavy, burdensome obligation without the Spirit's help. If evangelism is my work, I stagger under the load and dread the task. But if evangelism is the work of God's loving Spirit, I am relieved of that awful pressure. Because God has assumed the responsibility for convicting people and drawing them to him, I am set free to be a relaxed human being in love with my Father and the life he has given me. I do not have to pressure people or manipulate decisions. I can be myself and trust the Spirit to use me as I am. Because a loving God is in control, my witness for him is not a dreaded obligation, but a privileged celebration.

Our attempts to influence others for Christ are futile apart from the ongoing work of the Spirit. He guides. He generates power. And he gives peace. We must lean on him.

Make Disciples

Jesus' command to us is to make disciples or "learners." The witness's task is not to get a person to join a church. The witness's responsibility is to hold up Christ and to invite a person to commit himself to a lifelong journey of obedience.

It is not too hard today to get people to "make decisions." It is quite a task, though, to persuade people that they should stay with those decisions and become serious learners. As one writer put it:

> It is not difficult . . . to get a person interested in the message of the gospel; it is terrifically difficult to sustain the interest. Millions of people in our culture make decisions for Christ, but there is a dreadful attrition rate. Many claim to have been born again, but the evidence for mature Christian discipleship is slim.[1]

The true witness understands the nature of Christian commitment and will continue to encourage and support those who have decided for Christ. He will pray for the new follower, prod him to find a church, listen to his questions, and teach him the fundamentals of biblical truth. The effective evangelist, then, is not the one who hops from soul to soul securing decisions, but the one who stays with converts until they become disciples.

Guard the Mystery

If we are not careful, our evangelistic endeavors can come to sound like directions for baking a cake. Mix in all the right ingredients and, "presto," one knows God and has eternal life. Sometimes we make God too common, too trite, and too mechanical. Fred Craddock writes, "A husband and wife take hours and days and years to know each other, and yet some would know God before the parking meter expires."[2] Our attitudes and our words must reveal a distaste for any approach to God which makes him knowable before the parking meter expires. He is awesome and holy and marvelously mysterious, and therein lies the intrigue. If God could be exhausted in four quick propositions or three Bible verses, he has little to offer modern people. But, since he is the Holy Other who can be hinted at only in words and symbols and stirrings in the soul, he is a Supreme Being who can reshape one's destiny.

I am making a plea for a certain type of mysticism. Today's Christian persuader needs to be part mystic, to sense the wonder of a God who cannot be totally comprehended or programmed. Frederick Buechner was right, I think, when he wrote:

> Religion as a word points essentially, I think, to that area of human experience where in one way or another man happens upon mystery as a summons to pilgrimage, a come-all-ye; where he is led to suspect the reality of splendors that he cannot name; where he senses meanings no less overwhelming because they can only be hinted at in myths and rituals, in foolish, left-handed games and cloudy novels; where in great laughter and certain silences he glimpses a destination that he can never know fully until he reaches it.[3]

Colin Morris has observed that "the case for Christianity set down in cold print bears as much or as little resemblance to the real thing as a railway time-table does to an actual journey."[4] And anyone who has tried to give verbal testimony to his relationship with Christ realizes that the spoken word fares little better than the written one. We simply cannot articulate the truths we have discovered or the joys we have felt.

But we try—in awkward, insufficient ways. We pass a book on to a friend or pray with a searcher or tell our experiences to a doubter. Or maybe we quote Scripture or hand out tracts; but behind those actions needs to be an attitude of reverent humility, a recognition of miracle and mystery. We live for God, and we speak of God because we sense that he loves us and has called us to be ambassadors. But we also guard the mystery of his being and thank him that he is bigger than we can even imagine.

Use "Body Language"

Body language is one of the psychological discoveries of our day. Psychologists tell us that our body postures and movements reveal our true feelings even more than our words do. We may often communicate our real selves through this body language.

In his book *The Outward Bound,* Vernard Eller used the term *body language* in a different way. He used the term to describe that which is communicated by the "body of Christ," the church. And Eller asserted that this "body language" is the best kind of evangelism. In the context of a loving, searching, and committed church, a person can "catch" the gospel message and be drawn to it.

I think he is right. Many times I have heard that "just inviting someone to church" is not evangelism. Preachers and writers chide us because we sidestep real evangelism and just invite people to attend our churches. What those preachers and writers fail to consider is that a warm, caring church is the most effective tool of evangelism imaginable. When we invite a friend to worship with us and that friend catches the Christlike spirit which exists in our church, a legitimate Christian witness is being offered. There, in that caring "body," a person is likely to see clearly the "Head," who is Jesus Christ.

Certainly, every church on the face of the earth has problems. Petty squabbles and misplaced priorities are part and parcel of every church I know of. No church has perfect "body language." But the struggling, flawed "body of Christ" is still the best vehicle of communication around. I'll take the church over radio, television, and newspaper everytime as an effective tool of evangelism.

Therefore, use that tool. Invite people to come to your church, and make sure the "body language" is right when they arrive there.

Today's Christians are in a predicament. They find themselves sandwiched between a Book which says to bear unashamedly a message and a world that has been so bombarded with messages that it has grown either apathetic or plain hostile to persuasion. The solution to the predicament, in my mind, is a commitment to a personal influence characterized by sensitive boldness. The people who will make an impact on a world growing deaf and disillusioned are the ones who are sensitive enough to "feel with" people and bold enough to suggest a remedy.

The eight ideas pulled from my mental scrapbook form the skeleton of an approach to Christian influence I feel would provide this sensitive boldness. In summary, the persons who will be redemptive lights in our society are the ones who (1) are excited about being Christians, (2) have dropped some definite theological anchors, (3) begin to witness where they are, (4) have a feel for people and a flexible approach, (5) lean on the Spirit for guidance, power, and peace, (6) focus on making disciples, (7) guard the mystery and the holiness of God, and (8) use the "body language" of the church as a tool of evangelism.

Being a herald of the gospel in today's world is no easy vocation. Perhaps it never has been. But as we head to an office filled with greed, or converse with materialistic neighbors, or read the headlines proclaiming more mass violence, we can be cheered and bolstered by one simple question. It is the one penned by Paul years ago and sent to people struggling in a pagan world: "If God be for us, who can be against us?" (Rom. 8:31, KJV).

Since God is really for us, and no one can defeat us, we can move out into our world and witness for our Lord with confidence. Will you determine now to make influencing others for Christ a top priority in your life?

Notes

1. Eugene Peterson, *A Long Obedience in the Same Direction* (Downers Grove, Illinois: Inter-Varsity Press, 1980), p. 12.

2. Fred B. Craddock, *Overhearing the Gospel* (Nashville: Abingdon Press, 1978), p. 36.

3. Frederick Buechner, *The Alphabet of Grace* (New York: Seabury Press, 1970), p. 75.

4. Colin Morris, *Bugles in the Afternoon* (Philadelphia: The Westminster Press, 1977), p. 39.

9
Commitment:
Miscellaneous Dabbling or Single Passion?

Ours is a peculiar age in which a person is admired for being specific in technology, science, or medicine and ridiculed for being specific in religious commitment. In the fields of technology, science, and medicine, the "generalist" is an antique; now everyone is a specialist. But when it comes to the spiritual realm, the specialist is an antique, and the "generalist" is praised.

In the spiritual realm, the "miscellaneous person" is now in vogue in our country. The "miscellaneous person" is the one who dabbles in much and commits to nothing. He knows some psychology, some theology, some sociology, and even some astrology. The "miscellaneous person" is a sort of jack-of-all-trades who has sampled a little bit of everything on the table of life but sadly has been filled with nothing.

This jack-of-all-trades approach to spirituality leaves the "miscellaneous person" uncommitted and emotionless. In the modern mentality, spiritual passion is synonymous with fanaticism and thus is shunned at all costs. Modern people now glorify the "sophisticated" individual who knows something about every entrée on the smorgasbord of spiritual solutions but is above feasting on any particular one.

In a world where the dabbler in spiritual things is praised, the biblical message comes as a revolting shock. It demands obedience to a specific Lord. It claims to have the one answer to humanity's dilemma. It demands a single-minded passion that makes a person look like a "fool for Christ's sake." The New Testament, with its insistence that Jesus is the way to life and God, sounds too narrow and too stringent for sophisticated moderners who merely want to dabble.

Jesus himself would not fit well in late twentieth-century America. He would be too single-minded for our society. He said he was *the* Way, *the* Truth, and *the* Life. He said his sole purpose was to do the will of his Father, and his death on a Roman cross verified the sincerity of that commitment. He directed his followers to seek first the kingdom of God and not to become preoccupied with other things. He even had the gall to declare that most people would never find the narrow way of personal commitment that leads to life. No, Jesus was not a "miscellaneous person," and he had no place in his kingdom for "miscellaneous people," either.

The apostle Paul, too, would be rejected today. He certainly was no "generalist" and was not afraid to admit that he was an out-and-out fool for Christ. To the Corinthian Christians, Paul wrote that he was determined to know nothing among them but Jesus Christ and him crucified. To the Philippians, he stated he was going to do only one thing—"Press toward the goal for the prize of the upward call of God in Christ Jesus" (3:14). He also expressed his life's passion to those Philippian Christians when he testified, "For to me, to live is Christ" (1:21). No, Paul would not fit well in contemporary America, for he was definitely not a sophisticated dabbler. He was, instead, a passionate man who gambled everything on a Galilean Carpenter.

The pressing question is, Who is right, the miscellaneous dabblers or the single-minded, passionate ones? Each person must answer that question for himself, but I for one will cast my lot with Jesus, Paul, and the biblical writers of old. I believe Ernest Campbell was on target when he wrote:

The man to be pitied is the man who believes in everything just a
little bit, the miscellaneous man who has never brought the
tattered fragments of his life under the command of a single voice,
or gathered his abilities around a single passion.[1]

I believe that if there is no cause for which a man is prepared
to put his life on the line, then the stopping of his heart is just a
belated announcement of a death which has already taken place. I
believe that a single-minded, passionate commitment to Jesus
Christ is the way to authentic, joyous living.

This entire book rests upon that commitment. The preceding eight chapters have dealt with distinct areas of life where the
Christian should be different from the rest of society. But those
eight specific decisions to be a biblical nonconformist rest upon
one all-encompassing decision. That decision is to forego random
nibbling and to eat from the Bread of life, Jesus Christ, with
reckless abandon.

If we do not continually make that all-inclusive commitment to Christ, we will never be biblical in the specifics of life.
Why would anyone want to make money a tool of love unless
there is a firm belief that "spiritual stuff" is more vital to life than
"material stuff," as Jesus taught. Without an allegiance to Christ
and his way, any sane person would join the frenzied push for
"success" and status. Christ makes a difference in our economic
lives.

Why would anyone choose to express power by being a
servant, unless that person had caught a glimpse of the crucified
Lord and understood what that cross meant? Without Christ and
his cross, we might as well push, shove, intimidate, dominate,
and scramble for the top like the rest of the world. Christ makes a
difference in our quest for power.

Why would any modern person dare to believe the Beatitudes, unless that person believed in the Preacher who spoke

them? His way to happiness—through poverty of spirit, mourning, meekness, mercy, and all the rest—is obviously out of step with the modern mood; but some people will try his way because they believe in *him* so strongly. Christ makes a difference about which road we travel to find joy.

Our commitment to Christ also affects our view of sex. Because of him, sex can never be a fleeting and cheap thrill. To the follower of Jesus, sex is a part of a sacred and special commitment of husband and wife to each other. He makes a vast difference in our thinking about the purpose of a sexual relationship.

Why not let the contemporary church succumb to the tactics and priorities of the world if Christ is not its founder and cornerstone? Why not worship institutional success if Christ is not Lord? Without strong commitment by individual Christians to reproduce Christ in today's world, the church will inevitably stumble into materialism, spectacularism, and compromise. Christ makes a difference in how we view the role of the church.

Without the truth of Christ, why not seek wholeness through psychology, success, or "sincerity"? Without him, why not pin our hopes for salvation on the encounter group or the job promotion or the latest helpful philosophy? Christ makes a difference in our quest for abundant life.

When it comes to thoughts of eternity, why not eat, drink, and be merry if tomorrow we're all going to be extinguished? But if Christ did die and then came triumphantly out of the grave, and if we have entrusted our lives into his care, shouldn't we have confidence that he can carry us home? Christ makes a difference in our hopes for life beyond death.

Finally, in a world of manipulation and sales gimmicks, who wants to be sensitive and loving? And in a world of apathy and timid selfishness, who wants to be bold and candid? The follower of Jesus does! Christ makes a difference in how we choose to exert our influence.

Do you see? Individual decisions to be true to Christ's teachings in different areas of life rest upon the foundation of the lordship of Christ. If we dabble a bit in worship or Bible study or ministry, we will never have the conviction to make those specific commitments. They will come only as we daily decide to let Jesus be Lord.

Though it sounds dogmatically blunt, I must assert that much our society teaches us is a lie. Much that we assume to be true is, in fact, false. It is a lie that money shows how much a person is worth. It is a lie that power is found in domination and control. It is a lie that happiness is found in seeking expensive pleasures. It is a lie that sex is a cheap thrill. It is a lie that a church is supposed to be successful like a department store. It is a lie that salvation can be found outside of Jesus Christ. It is a lie that there is no eternity. And it is a lie that it is wrong to lovingly influence others for Christ.

Our only hope is to recognize the falseness of some of the world's gospel and to step to the beat of a different Drummer. Let us pray with Eugene Peterson,

Rescue me from the lies of advertisers who claim to know what I need and what I desire, from the lies of entertainers who promise a cheap way to joy, from the lies of politicians who pretend to instruct me in power and morality, from the lies of psychologists who offer to shape my behavior and my morals so that I will live long, happily, and successfully, from the lies of religionists who "heal the wounds of this people lightly," from the lies of moralists who pretend to promote me to the office of captain of my fate, from the lies of pastors who "leave the commandment of God, and hold fast the tradition of men" (Mk. 7:8). Rescue me from the person who tells me of life and omits Christ, who is wise in the ways of the world and ignores the movement of the Spirit.[2]

As we try to discern the truth in the midst of a confusing multitude of claims, let me mention three things that perhaps can prod us to commit ourselves unreservedly to Christ. Hopefully, these three truths can cut through the confusion and help us cast our lives on him.

Where You Look Determines What You Become

Nathaniel Hawthorne's story "The Great Stone Face" tells of a young man named Ernest who gazed for years at a face nature had carved into the side of a mountain. Eventually, Ernest's face assumed the same characteristics as the great stone face at which he gazed. The truth of Hawthorne's story is one we need to remember: where we look determines what we become.

Whatever claims our attention, whatever occupies our minds, whatever captures our interest will shape us into its image. If we look greedily and longingly at financial success, we will become materialists. If we gaze at pornography, we will become lustful. If we focus on violence, we will become violent. If we concentrate on self, we will become selfish. Our lives are always molded by those ideas and people at which we look.

That is why the writer of the Book of Hebrews challenged us to keep "fixing our eyes on Jesus, the author and perfecter of faith" (12:2). As we fix our eyes on him, as we learn about him, as we try to adopt his priorities, we are gradually fashioned into his image. Like Ernest, we are transformed into the likeness of the one at which we gaze. As we fix our eyes on Jesus, the process of change is always set in motion within us.

Of course, we are never forced to look at him. There is a wide variety of alluring people and philosophies vying for our attention. Where we focus our gaze is strictly a matter of personal choice. But amid the din of voices beckoning to us, there still rings the voice of the Galilean Carpenter offering his simple, but costly, invitation: "Follow me."

Those who say yes to him will still have some days of discouragement and confusion. Saying yes to Jesus does not guarantee problem-free living. What it *does* guarantee is change and personal growth. Those who fix their eyes on him will inevitably start to become like him.

But even if we choose to look elsewhere, the truth remains constant: where we choose to look determines what we become.

What You Do Determines How You Feel

We usually think the reverse is true. We tend to think that how we feel determines what we do. That is, we let our feelings dictate our actions. We try to "feel" our way into a new way of acting. As Christians, we cling to the notion that one of these days we're going to "get the right feeling," then we'll give, pray, serve, and love gladly and freely. So, we sit in our cozy houses and churches waiting for that special, heaven-sent feeling that will transform us into dynamic saints.

We could have a long wait. It is even distinctly possible that "the feeling" will never come. Notice sometime how little the Bible has to say about feeling a certain way. We are never told, in the written Word, to have goosebumps or spine-tingling chills. The stress is never on feeling; it is on obedience. We are commissioned to obey God. Whether we happen to "feel" like obeying him is beside the point.

This stress of obedience is a note that needs to be sounded in a society that is extremely feeling oriented. If we would take our obedience seriously, we would discover an amazing truth: what we do determines how we feel. In other words, the feelings usually come *after* obedience, not before. If we wait for the right feeling before we obey, we might wait forever without doing any thing. But if we will seek to obey God regardless of our feelings, we will probably find the joyous feeling we desire. It is easier to act our way into a new manner of feeling than it is to feel our way into a new style of acting.

Some ways have been mentioned in which Christians are to be different from others. Some specific differences have been highlighted. But if we wait to "feel" like putting these things into practice, most likely we will never do any of them. If we wait until we feel like using our money as a tool of love, for instance, we will never do it. Or if we wait until we get goosebumps over servanthood, we will never serve anyone. I think we must act first, and then see if joy comes.

Remember this, then, as you consider the extent of your commitment to Christ: what you do determines how you feel.

When You Start Determines How Far You Go

In terms of our Christian growth, we reap what we sow. While we might like to think that we can become "super saints" by magic, it just doesn't work that way. As Paul said, we have to "work out our salvation." We are to work out what he has worked in. We have to "press toward the mark" that God has placed before us. Of course, our deeds do not earn God's favor. Of course, grace comforts us on the journey. Of course, God loves us even when we stumble. But we will never be transformed into the likeness of Christ without some personal struggle, some personal discipline, and some personal initiative. When we start the journey toward Christlikeness determines how far we go.

The Christian distinctives I have discussed in this book can actually discourage us from even beginning the journey. Face-to-face with painful biblical truths, all of us realize how far we have to go in our spiritual pilgrimages. "Working out our salvation" can be depressing if we look at all of the changes we should make.

But rather than despairing over our shortcomings, we can begin now to tackle just one area where we are especially weak. We can find one place in our lives that needs attention and go to work there. After all, God wants us to be growing toward perfection, Christlikeness.

The ancient Chinese proverb says, "A journey of a thousand miles must begin with a single step." The journey to authentic, biblical Christianity begins with step too. And when we take that first step will determine, to a large extent, how far we go.

In the light of the three truths I have mentioned, three personal and probing questions about our Christian commitment come into view. First, who or what has captured our gaze? Second, must we have a certain "high" feeling before we can act upon the Bible's commands? Third, will there ever be a better time than now to make following Christ the passion of our lives?

John Baillie once wrote, "I am sure that the point of the road that most requires to be illuminated is the point where it forks."[3] It has been my purpose in this book to illumine, even faintly, the point where the road forks, the point where truth and falsehood diverge, the point where one path becomes narrow and the other becomes wide. In short, I have tried to show where Scripture and society part company.

But after some light has been shed, each one of us must decide which path to take. Would you dare to take "the [road] less traveled by"? Would you choose Christ and become a Christian nonconformist? Would you make serious discipleship a matter of choice?

The pressure each of us faces to be conformists is enormmous. It takes courage to be different. But let us determine not to be like everyone else. Life is more than eating, sleeping, working, reproducing, and dying. Life can be God, love, wonder, purpose, creativity, and deeply caring relationships. Let us stake our lives upon Christ and then love him unreservedly. Let us be transformed people today and then trust our Lord to continue this transformation into eternity.

Notes

1. Ernest T. Campbell, *Locked in a Room with Open Doors* (Waco: Word Books, 1974), p. 43.

2. Peterson, p. 23.

3. John Baillie, *Invitation to Pilgrimage* (Grand Rapids: Baker Book House, 1942), p. 8.